Young people and crime

by
John Graham
and Benjamin Bowling

A Research and Planning Unit Report

Home Office
Research and
Statistics
Department

London: Home Office

Home Office Research Studies

The Home Office Research Studies are reports on research undertaken by or on behalf of the Home Office. They cover the range of subjects for which the Home Secretary has responsibility. Titles in the series are listed at the back of this report (copies are available from the address on back cover). Other publications produced by the Research and Planning Unit include Research Findings (which are summaries of research projects), the Research Bulletin (published twice each year) and the annual Research Programme.

The Research and Statistics Department

The Department consists of the Research and Planning Unit, three Statistics Divisions, the Programme Development Unit and the Economics Unit.

 The Research and Statistics Department is an integral part of the Home Office, serving the Ministers and the department itself, its services, Parliament and the public through research, development and statistics. Information and knowledge from these sources informs policy development and the management of programmes; their dissemination improves wider public understanding of matters of Home Office concern.

First published 1995

Application for reproduction should be made to the Information Section, Research and Planning Unit, Home Office, 50 Queen Anne's Gate, London SW1H 9AT.

Foreword

Much research has attempted to illuminate the reasons why young people engage in criminal activities, but little attention has focused on why some young offenders stop offending whilst others go on offending well into adulthood. This study looks at offending by young people during the period of transition from childhood to adulthood and assesses whether, on the basis of self-report data, young offenders do actually grow out of crime and if so, why. The findings are both expected and unexpected. The research shows that female offenders do indeed grow out of crime by the time they reach their mid-twenties, but that many male offenders do not. It shows that young female offenders who complete their education, leave home, set up their own independent lifestyle and begin to form families of their own have a high chance of desisting from offending. For male offenders, however, these life events do not seem to have the same effect. For them, the risks faced during the period of transition between childhood and adulthood are considerable and for them, the chances of desisting from offending once they start are significantly less than for females.

The study concludes with a wide ranging discussion of possible strategies for preventing the onset of, and promoting desistance from, offending. These strategies include strengthening families and schools, preparing young people for leaving home, supporting the formation of new families and harnessing formal and informal sources of social control. A number of areas for further research are also highlighted.

ROGER TARLING
Head of the Research and Planning Unit
November 1995

Acknowledgements

We would like to thank a large number of people who have assisted us with this report. First and foremost, we would like to express our gratitude to MORI, and in particular Kai Rudat, for overseeing the national survey and to the team of interviewers who went out, often at night, in search of the young people who answered our questions. We would also like to thank David Farrington and Clive Payne for their expert advice on the statistical analysis, Alec Ross and Andrew Zurawan for their invaluable assistance with data preparation and analysis, Stephen Farrall for his assistance with the in-depth interviews and during the early stages of the research and Julie Vennard, Hilary Jackson, Brian Kinney, Pat Mayhew, Malcolm Ramsey, Natalie Aye-Maung, Roger Tarling and Marian Fitzgerald for their constructive comments on earlier drafts of the report.

Most importantly, we would also like to express our gratitude to all those young people who gave up their time to talk to our interviewers, especially those who we interviewed twice, and to the parents and guardians who gave us their consent and allowed us into their homes.

JOHN GRAHAM

BEN BOWLING

Contents

		Page
Foreword		iii
Acknowledgements		vi
Contents		v
Summary		ix
1	Introduction.	1
	Crime and the transition from childhood to adulthood	2
	Previous research on why young people start to offend	4
	Previous research on desistance from offending	5
	Research design	6
2	Patterns of offending	11
	Participation in offending	11
	Frequency of offending	18
	Summary	21
3	Age and offending	23
	Age of onset	23
	Participation in offending by age and sex.	24
	Frequency of offending by age and sex	28
	Summary and discussion	29

4   Initiating offending: why do some young people start to offend   31

Defining an "offender" for the purposes of explanatory analysis   32

Family background and starting to offend   33

School factors   39

Delinquent peers   42

Modelling the onset of offending   43

Adverse factors and delinquency   47

Summary and conclusions   48

5   The transition to adulthood and desistance from offending   51

Defining "desisters"   52

Social development and the transition from childhood to adulthood   54

Social development and desistance from offending   56

Desistance among different age groups   58

Desistance from different types of offence   59

Modelling desistance from offending   60

Discussion and conclusions   64

6   Explaining desistance from offending   67

Methodology   67

Disassociation from delinquent peers   70

Forming stable relationships and having children   72

Acquiring a sense of direction   76

Realising in time or learning the hard way   78

Maturity, responsibility and moral development   80

7   Discussion and conclusions   83

        Preventing the onset of offending   85

        Encouraging desistance from offending   93

        Some future directions for research   103

Appendix A. Survey design and method   105

Appendix B. List of criminal offences included   109

Appendix C. Supplementary tables: individual offences   111

Appendix D. Multivariate analysis   117

Appendix E. The effects of age on desistance   125

References   127

Publications   135

Summary

The study aimed to provide an estimate of the extent, frequency and nature of self-reported offending among 14- to 25- year olds in England and Wales, to establish the reasons why some young people start to offend, and what influences those young offenders who desist from offending to sustain a non- criminal lifestyle.

Exploring these areas involved a two-stage research strategy. Firstly a national random sample of 1,721 young people aged 14 to 25 (plus a booster sample of 808 young people from ethnic minorities) were interviewed about their background, their family life, their school experiences and aspects of their current lifestyle. Respondents were asked to admit whether they had ever committed one of a list of 23 criminal offences (see Appendix B) or used controlled drugs. Those who had ever committed at least one offence were asked at what age they committed each type of offence for the first time and whether they had also committed an offence within the past year (1992). "Active" offenders were asked, amongst other things, how many offences they had committed during the past year and for details about their most recent offences.

The second stage of the research involved life-history interviews with 21 "desisters" – young people identified as having offended in the past but not within the previous year. Through these retrospective accounts, it was possible to track events over time and identify the influences, conditions and circumstances which ultimately led to desistance from offending.

Chapter 2 describes the extent and nature of criminal offending and Chapter 3 looks at changes in these patterns of offending by age. Chapter 4 provides an analysis of why some young people start committing offences, whilst Chapter 5 examines the notion that offenders "grow out of " crime with age and identifies the main factors associated with desistance from offending. Chapter 6 explores the process of desistance through in-depth interviews with a sub-sample of desisters. Chapter 7 draws out the conclusions of the study and discusses a range of policy options. The key findings are outlined below.

The extent and nature of offending

The survey of self-reported offending – that which respondents admitted to in the interview – provides an estimate of offending unaffected by selection and processing by the criminal justice system. It estimates how many young people offend, when they start, how serious the offences are and how frequently they are committed. It allows comparisons to be made by sex, age, class and ethnic origin. The main findings are:

- Involvement in offending is widespread among this age group – one in two males and one in three females admitted to ever committing an offence – but the majority of offenders commit no more than one or two minor offences. Property offending is more common than violent offending by a factor of about two for males and three for females.

- One in four males and one in eight females admitted committing an offence in 1992; of these, about a quarter of male offenders and one in ten female offenders admitted committing more than five offences. Overall, about three per cent of offenders accounted for approximately a quarter of all offences.

- The use of drugs is widespread amongst young people; every other male and every third female have used drugs at some time in their lives. Most drug use is confined to cannabis, which is consumed regularly (at least once a week) by one in three male and one in five female users. Drugs other than cannabis are consumed less regularly, although 13 per cent of male users and 19 per cent of female users did so at least once a week.

- Asians – those of Indian, Pakistani and Bangladeshi origin – have significantly lower rates of offending than whites and Afro-Caribbeans who have very similar rates of offending. Whites are slightly more likely to use drugs than Afro-Caribbeans, who in turn are more likely to use drugs than Asians.

- The most common or peak age at which young people *start* to offend and take cannabis is 15 for both males and females. This is one year later than the peak age of onset for truancy and running away from home,[1] and one year earlier than the most common age at which young people begin to take drugs other than cannabis.

---

1   Those who were classified as having run away from home were those who had spent at least one night away from home without the knowledge of their parents.

- The ratio of male:female self-reported offending for juveniles is nearly 1:1, but this increases to 4:1 for older teenagers and 11:1 for those in their early twenties. The peak age of offending for males is 21 and for females 16.

- For females, the rate of self-reported offending declines substantially after the mid-teens. By their early twenties, the rate of offending amongst females is five times lower than among female juveniles. In contrast, the rate of self-reported offending for males increases with age up to 18 and remains at the same level into the mid-twenties. Participation in property offending actually *increases* with age suggesting that, as they grow older, some males may switch from relatively risky property offences, such as shoplifting and burglary, to less visible and thus less detectable forms of property crime, such as fraud[2] and theft from the workplace. However, serious offending decreases for both males and females as they reach their mid-twenties, as does frequency of offending.

Starting to offend

By comparing "non-offenders" (those who had *never* offended) with "offenders" (those who have offended at some time in the past) it is possible to explore whether there are statistical associations between offending and such factors as social class, family size, structure and relationships, schooling and peer group affiliations. This provides a basis for explaining why some young people start to offend while others do not.

In common with other self-report studies (and in contrast to studies based on recorded crime data) this study found only a weak relationship between social class and offending and this relationship disappeared after controlling for family and school variables. Similarly, young people living in larger families were no more likely to offend than those from smaller families. However, young people living with both natural parents were found to be less likely to offend than those living with one parent or in a step family. The higher rate of offenders from single parent families was found to be statistically associated with less parental supervision, a greater likelihood of a poor relationship with at least one parent and greater poverty.[3] A poor relationship with at least one parent and lower levels of parental supervision accounted for the higher levels of offending by children living in step families.

---

2   Fraud comprises "used or sold a cheque book, credit card, cash point card (ATM card) belonging to you or someone else so that they could steal money from a bank account or claimed on an insurance policy, an expenses form, a tax return or a social security benefit form that you knew to be incorrect in order to make money" (see Appendix B).

3   It was not possible to establish the standard of living of parents and poverty here is therefore measured in terms of the degree to which the respondent cannot afford a range of essentials, namely food, clothing and a place to live (for self and family).

Both males and females who were less attached to their families were more likely to offend than those who were relatively content at home. Those whose relationships with their parents led them to running away from home (prior to the age of 16) were particularly likely to offend as were males who got on badly with their fathers. For both males and females, low parental supervision was also found to be strongly related to offending (irrespective of family structure) and young people with friends or siblings in trouble with the police were much more likely to offend than others.

Females who disliked school, or who rated their performance below or well below average, were more likely to offend than those who liked school or rated their performance more positively. For males, neither their attitude towards nor their performance at school were found to be related to their starting to offend. However, those who truanted from school, especially those who did so regularly, and those who had been excluded from school, were much more likely to offend than others.

Multi-variate analysis indicated that the strongest correlates of onset of offending are contact with delinquent peers, truancy and low parental supervision. For males, having delinquent siblings and being excluded from school were also strong correlates of offending, as were low attachment to family and school for females. The two most important predictors of offending – truancy and low parental supervision – are both strongly dependent upon the quality of parent-child relationships. The more of these adverse circumstances young people experience during their childhoods, the more they are likely to offend. Over 80 per cent of young males and over 60 per cent of young females who experienced four or five of the most powerful influences on offending were actually offenders.

Desistance from offending

To find out whether young people grow out of crime and if so why, they were asked a number of questions relating to the main life events which characterise the transition from childhood to adulthood. These included completing full-time education, taking up stable employment, leaving home, getting married/forming a stable partnership, staying in to look after children and taking responsibility for themselves and others. On the basis of these criteria, many young people had not completed the transition to adulthood by their mid-twenties. On all of these measures, males were found to lag behind females. If it is true that young people grow out of crime, then many will not do so by their mid-twenties simply by virtue of the fact that they (especially males) have not been able to grow up. To test this, an analysis of the relationship between these life events and desistence from offending was undertaken.

Females who successfully made the transition to adulthood – for example had completed full-time education, left home and formed a new family unit – were significantly more likely to have desisted from offending than those who had not. For males, however, passing these landmarks had no such effect. For them, the only factors which influenced their chances of desistance were continuing to live at home into their twenties, being successful at school and avoiding the criminogenic influences of associating with other offenders (friends, partners and siblings), using drugs (particularly hard drugs) and heavy drinking. Some of these factors (in particular continuing to live at home and associating with other offenders) were found to be strongly related to the quality of relationships with parents.

Through interviews with individual desisters, it was possible to track events over time and identify the influences, conditions and circumstances which ultimately led to desistance from offending. The interviews indicated that for young women, desistance tends to occur abruptly and consciously as they leave home, leave school, form stable partnerships and have children. For males, however, desistance was found to be more gradual and intermittent, with attempts to stop often thwarted by events or changes in circumstances. For them, the positive effects of personal and social developments tended to be outweighed by the more powerful influences of the peer group. Other factors which promote desistance are finding a sense of direction and meaning in life, realising the consequences of one's actions on others and learning that crime doesn't pay.

Policy implications

The implications for policy fall into two parts. The first is concerned with preventing individuals from ever starting to offend and the second with finding ways to encourage offenders to desist. Based on what emerged from the study as the strongest influences on offending and desistance from offending during the transition to adulthood, policies are discussed strengthening individual families and schools, forming family-school partnerships, resisting the powerful criminogenic effects of involvement in delinquent peer groups and preparing young people for leaving home, forming new families and achieving independence and a sense of adult responsibility.

Preventing the onset of offending

Many of the policies for strengthening families are concerned with improving intra-familial relationships and parental supervision through parent training, the provision of open access family centres, support groups for parents of teenagers, family preservation and a range of measures for improving the awareness of parents of the risks of adolescence and the implications of offending behaviour for their children. Specific measures for single parents and step families are also recommended.

Policies for strengthening schools are related to reducing and preventing truancy and school exclusions through, first and foremost, the promotion of effective schooling and building on recent government initiatives to discourage truancy and school exclusions. Specific measures include exploring and setting up schemes for improving liaison with parents, setting up school support teams and ensuring schools take full responsibility for disaffected pupils.

Developing family-school partnerships is recommended as a way of synergising the potential benefits from each to produce a whole greater than the sum of the two parts. A number of specific measures are suggested to, on the one hand, encourage parents to become more involved in their child's education and school life and, on the other hand, to encourage teachers to communicate more often and more effectively with parents. These include the use of home-school agreements on attendance and behaviour, involving parents in primary-to-secondary induction, providing home-to-school telephone links, encouraging teachers to make home visits and establishing joint approaches to discipline, supervision and control. It is suggested that primary schools in particular could form the central foci for community-based criminality prevention strategies.

Encouraging desistance from offending

For females, encouraging the natural processes of personal and social maturation will foster desistance from offending, but for males, these processes are not only delayed compared with females, but do not seem to influence desistance to any significant degree. Continuing to live at home protects young male offenders from persisting with crime. For those young men who leave home during their teenage years, a range of measures could be implemented to prepare them better for life in the outside world. Suggestions include bridging schemes, such as the French system of foyers, which provide temporary accommodation coupled with training and employment; better preparation for early fatherhood and for parenting teenagers; and encouraging fathers as well as other male adults to support and "parent" young adult males in the community and provide responsible masculine role models.

Preventing substance abuse

Leffert and Petersen (1995), in their contribution to a European Study Group's analysis of trends in psychosocial disorders in young people, concluded that young people today face more serious hazards than their predecessors in making the transition from childhood to adulthood. They conclude, in particular, that the heavy use of drugs and alcohol carries with it an increased risk of criminal behaviour (see, also, Sampson and Laub, 1993). The findings from this study support their conclusions. Where young male offenders begin to indulge in alcohol and drug misuse, they are likely to become embedded in a criminal lifestyle from which it becomes increasingly difficult to disengage. Young male offenders – those aged 13 or 14 – therefore need to be specifically targeted for substance abuse prevention if they are to avoid this pathway. More generally, substance abuse prevention programmes based in schools and local communities which involve parents and older peers as role models are recommended. Since the antecedents of substance abuse and delinquency are very similar, locally co-ordinated programmes of prevention for young people at risk of either (or both) would avoid duplication of effort and funding and improve the prospect of later desistance.

Harnessing informal to formal sources of social control

The criminal justice system clearly plays a central role in encouraging desistance. Fear of being caught, of acquiring a criminal record, of being labelled and of ending up in prison all contribute to desistance for some individuals. Little evidence was found that young male offenders develop a moral conscience which may act to inhibit their offending as they grow older. Given the widespread involvement of young people in crime and drug misuse it is suggested that, to be more effective, the criminal justice system could be encouraged to harness the more powerful sources of social control exercised by families, schools and neighbours. The model of restorative justice, as practised by Family Group Courts in New Zealand, in which the power of family attachments to induce a sense of shame, atonement and responsibility plays a central role, is suggested as one possible way of achieving this.

1 Introduction

In the Autumn of 1992, the House of Commons Home Affairs Select Committee set up an Inquiry into issues affecting juvenile offenders as a result of public concern about the level of juvenile crime and the inability of the criminal justice system to deal adequately with it. The Committee's task was severely hampered by the conflicting evidence it received on trends in the incidence of juvenile crime. In essence, the Committee was sceptical about whether the statistics on juvenile crime accurately reflected the real situation and felt they simply obscured the incidence and prevalence of offending and trends over time. The Report of the Committee went on to recommend "that the Home Office should consider how any improvements to overall juvenile crime statistics could be made which would enable more informed policy decisions to be taken". In addition to the problems encountered over the accuracy of recorded statistics, the Committee also uncovered demand for additional forms of data and a more informed debate. The National Association of Probation Officers (NAPO) and the National Association for the Care and Resettlement of Offenders (NACRO) called for extra information to be made available so that trends in juvenile offending could more easily be identified and the Association of Metropolitan Authorities requested further research into how offending varies with age. This study goes a considerable way to meeting these demands by providing, for the first time in this country, a national representative survey of self-report offending by young people broken down by age, sex and ethnic origin. The design allows the survey to be repeated every few years so that trends in offending by this age group can also be identified.

A second issue identified by the Home Affairs Select Committee concerned the limitations of the criminal justice system in responding to the problem of crime and the resultant necessity of "investing in identifying and eliminating the causes of crime and in crime prevention." The committee went on to point out that "it is equally important to stop young people from ascending the ladder of crime once they have stepped on the bottom rung." This, the committee concluded, "is clearly preferable to paying for the damage once it has been done." In response to this, the present study provides an analysis of the reasons why young people start to offend and why some of them stop and on the basis of this information, develops policies for preventing crime and criminality. The main aims of the study can therefore be summarised as follows:

(i)   To provide a national estimate of offending by 14- to 25- year olds broken down by age, sex and ethnic origin.

(ii) To provide a base line estimate of the prevalence and frequency of offending by this age group from which trend data can be generated.

(iii) To analyse changes in patterns of offending within the context of the changes which occur in the lives of young people as they progress from childhood to adulthood.

(iv) To establish the reasons why some young people start to offend.

(v)   To establish which young offenders desist from offending and what the processes are which lead to desistance and sustain a non-criminal lifestyle.

Crime and the transition from childhood to adulthood

The period in which young people move from childhood to adulthood is a critical one in the development of an individual. Commonly referred to as adolescence, it is a period characterised by uncertainty, the need to develop a personal identity and, most importantly, the establishment of material and emotional independence and the status of adulthood. Physical maturity is an important signifier of adulthood but in addition to this, it requires taking responsibility for oneself, managing one's own affairs and learning to enjoy new freedoms without neglecting one's duties towards and responsibilities for others (DES, 1983).

Age alone is not a consistent signifier of adulthood. In UK law there is no single dividing line between children and adults; rather, adult status is gained slowly over many years. Sexual intercourse and marriage are legal at 16 (also the age of responsibility for tax purposes); driving a car is legal at 17; voting rights are gained at 18 when the consumption of alcohol in public houses also becomes legal; homosexual relationships for males are currently legal at 21. In practice, however, young people acquire the attributes of adulthood at different ages, and the above are merely signposts on the way.

At the beginning of the transition to adulthood young people begin to move away from the protective embrace of their parents and become increasingly dependent on their peers for satisfying many of their personal, emotional and social needs. This is also a period during which the boundaries of right and wrong are tested to the full and risks are undertaken in the pursuit of excitement and status, that are unprecedented in any other stage of the human life cycle. Indeed adolescence is characterised by the highest levels of involvement in offending of any period throughout the entire life-span.

According to recorded statistics on offending, young people aged 14 to 25 accounted for 60 per cent of all indictable offences in 1993. More than one-third of male adults will have been convicted of a standard list offence by their mid-thirties (Home Office, 1993). Since the chances of being appre-hended and convicted are small – about three in every 100 offences result in a caution or a conviction (Home Office, 1993) – it is perhaps not surprising that a majority of young people will commit an offence at some time during this period.

Recorded statistics on offending also suggest that the peak age of offending (measured in terms of cautions and convictions) is 15 for females and 18 for males (Home Office, 1993) and that after these peak ages young people begin to grow out of crime (see also Rutherford, 1992). However, while it seems likely that the offending careers of young people, and in particular whether they continue to offend or not following the peak age of offending, will be closely related to changes in their personal and social circumstances, there has been little research on how these changes influence desistance from offending and the maintenance of a non-criminal lifestyle among young people who once offended.

Most research on the transition to adulthood has concluded that leaving school, gaining employment, getting married and becoming a parent are the major life events that characterise the transition to adulthood (see, for example, Hogan & Astone, 1986). This study is concerned principally with the social and developmental aspects of the transition from childhood to adulthood, and in particular, those that may account for desistance from offending. For the purposes of this study, the status of adulthood is charac-terised by the following features:

- Completing compulsory education

- Gaining stable employment

- Being in a marriage/partner relationship

- Becoming a parent

- Leaving the parental home and setting up one's own home

- Taking responsibilities for oneself and for others

- Gaining financial independence and a degree of autonomy.

In order to explore the influence of these factors on desistance from offending, this study looked at the extent to which young men and women make this transition by the age of 25, at what age these transitional landmarks are passed (if at all) and how passing through these landmarks is related to changes in patterns of offending and desistance from offending.

Previous research on why young people start to offend

This is not the place to review the extensive literature on why people start to offend (see for example, Farrington, 1994a; Tarling, 1993; Home Affairs Committee, 1993). However, it is worth summarising the findings of one of the most detailed British studies of delinquency ever carried out – the Cambridge Study of Delinquent Development – which had similar aims to this study. Using both self-report and official data, this prospective longitudinal survey followed the fortunes of 411 white working class males born in 1953 in an Inner London Borough (West and Farrington 1973, 1977). It attempted to describe the development of criminal behaviour, predict who becomes delinquent and explain why most teenage male offenders desist from offending as they reach adulthood.

The main findings were that one-fifth were convicted of offences as juveniles (i.e. before age 17), a quarter by the age of 18 and a third by the age of 25. Half of those convicted of offences as juveniles were also frequent self-reported delinquents, whilst half of those who admitted to offences had not been convicted of an offence. The most important independent predictors of offending were found to be poverty, poor parenting, parental and sibling criminality, school problems and anti-social behaviour. The best predictor of delinquency was found to be early troublesome behaviour at age eight to 10. Marriage, girlfriends and a reduction in the influence of delinquent peers were found to be related to desistance from offending.

Unfortunately, the Cambridge Study of Delinquent Development does not include females or ethnic minorities and its findings are based on a relatively small, unrepresentative sample, which cannot be necessarily generalised to the nation as a whole. Furthermore, the children in the study began to offend in the late 1960s and 1970s, a period which is somewhat different from the 1980s. Today, rates of offending are much higher and the social and economic conditions under which young people grow up have changed considerably. Nevertheless, much of what the Cambridge Study of Delinquent Development discovered about why some young people start to offend is confirmed in this study

Previous research on desistance from offending

Despite the intuitive appeal of the notion that young people start to offend as they enter adolescence and move away from the supervision and control of their parents but in time 'grow out' of crime, there is a paucity of research evidence to confirm this. Research on desistance from offending has either focused on older adults (see, for example, Shover, 1983 and 1985) or exclusively on males (Rand, 1987; Sampson and Laub, 1993). Furthermore, with the exception of the Cambridge Study in Delinquent Development (West, 1982; Farrington 1994b) and one or two ethnographic studies (see, for example, Parker, 1976), there has been no other empirical research on desistance from offending amongst young people in England and Wales.

An American study of 106 male offenders (Rand 1987) found that marriage and vocational training in the armed forces were correlated with desistance. Those who were co-habiting (but not married) or were members of youth gangs were less likely to desist. Fatherhood, military service and college training had no effect on desistance. Shover (1983 and 1985), looking at US male ex-prisoners in their 30s and 40s, found that commitment to a person or a job or both led to the development of a daily routine which consequently left little or no time for criminal involvement. Most recently Sampson and Laub (1993), using data from the Glueck's 1940s longitudinal study of delinquency amongst young males, concluded that job stability, cohesive marital attachment and military service were the most important influences on desistance. Negative influences were prolonged incarceration, heavy drinking and job instability. However, the data used in this study is over fifty years old and the dangers of transferring the findings of American research in general and this study in particular to this country need to be heeded.

In England and Wales, Parker's ethnographic study of "the boys" – a group of young men involved in car-radio theft among other things – identified a number of pressures against criminal involvement. These included the splintering of the peer group, the development of partnerships, spending time with partners and children, taking responsibility for rent and house-keeping and fear of being caught and punished. Knight and West (1975), quoted in Tarling (1993), found that some of those who desisted in the Cambridge Study of Delinquent Development did so as a result of no longer associating with delinquent friends. This, it is suggested, may be due to consciously deciding not to get involved in situations which may lead to crime or fortuitously as a consequence of moving away or, for older offenders, marrying a non-delinquent woman.

Research design

The aims of the project were addressed using a household survey which collected data on self reported offending and respondents' backgrounds and personal and social development. A national random sample comprising 893 respondents plus a further 828 respondents randomly sampled from areas of high victimisation produced a nationally representative sample of 1,721 (after weighting). An ethnic minority booster sample, used only to make comparisons among different ethnic groups, comprised an additional 808 cases giving a total sample size of 2,529 (see Appendix A for a full description of the research design, sampling frame and methodology). The fifth aim of the study – the processes leading to desistance from offending – was further investigated through a series of in-depth, follow-up interviews with a sub-sample of respondents from the main survey.

The self report method

The data used most often to gauge the extent and nature of crime and to investigate the characteristics of criminals are "official" records – crimes recorded by the police, and persons found guilty of, or cautioned for, a criminal offence. These statistics on offending and offenders are the end point of a process consisting of the commission of a criminal offence, reporting to the police, the detection of an offender, the decision to charge with a criminal offence, the decision to prosecute, and the finding of guilt and conviction in a criminal court. It is estimated that around two per cent of all crimes committed result in the conviction of an offender (Home Office, 1993), so inferences about offending and offenders based on individuals who pass through the criminal justice system may not apply to unrecorded offending or undetected offenders (Tarling, 1993). Surveys of victims provide fuller estimates of unrecorded crime but add little to our knowledge of the characteristics of offenders or their offending.

Surveys of self-reported offending – that which respondents will admit to in an interview – constitute a third approach to measuring the extent and nature of offending and are able to cover offences both detected and undetected, irrespective of whether there is an identifiable victim. For example self-report surveys can identify offences directed against business (such as shoplifting and fraud), carrying weapons, serious motoring offences and the use and sale of controlled drugs. Such surveys avoid some of the inadequacies and biases inherent in the compilation of public official records and provide information on offending and offenders unaffected by selection and processing by the police and criminal justice system (Hindelang *et al.*, 1981).

In this study, a national random sample of 1,721 young people aged 14 to 25 (hitherto referred to as the core sample), together with a booster sample of 808 respondents from ethnic minorities of the same age, were asked whether they had ever committed a range of offences (ranging from vandalism to serious property and violent crimes). Those who said they had offended were asked at what age they committed each type of offence for the first time and whether they had also committed the offence within the past year (1992). This data allowed estimates to be made of how many people offend, when they start, how serious the offences are and how frequently they are committed. Comparisons are made by sex, age, class and ethnic origin. To check whether the national sample was representative of 14- to 25- year olds as a whole, comparisons were made with other national data sources. Overall, the sample was found to slightly over-represent younger respondents, students, the unemployed and those on YTS (see Appendix A). The survey also provides information on whether offenders do actually desist from offending and at what age. (As a cross-sectional survey it does not, of course, provide information on inter-generational changes.)

Active offenders – those stating that they had offended within the last year – were not only asked how many times they had done so, but also to provide further details in respect of the most recent occasion, such as whether they were caught and what happened as a result. They were also asked whether or not they thought they would offend again in the future. Data were also collected on the likelihood of coming to the attention of parents, teachers and the police for offences of different types and levels of seriousness, but the findings are not presented here.

The data on past and present offending enabled a comparison between non-offenders (those who had never offended) and offenders (those who have offended at some time in the past). Comparing these two groups in terms of age, sex, class and a range of other independent variables such as family background and relationships, schooling and peer group affiliations, allows factors which have statistical associations with offending to be identified. This provided a basis for developing explanations for why some young people start to offend while others do not.

Having explored some of the factors which help to explain why some young people start to offend, the study investigates the factors which distinguish active offenders (those who offended in 1992) from desisters (those who have offended in the past but have stopped for a year at least – see Chapter 5 for a more precise definition). The factors which form the focus of the analysis comprise the main aspects of the transition to adulthood, such as leaving home and establishing an independent living space, leaving full-time education and taking up employment, and taking on the responsibilities of a partner and children. By comparing active offenders with desisters in terms of whether or not they have passed each of these specific landmarks, an assessment can be made of whether any reduction in offending can be attributed to growing out of crime.

Limitations of the self report method

Although the self-report method is accepted as a valid and reasonably reliable means of measuring the extent and distribution of criminal acts, and of investigating the characteristics of offenders, it has a number of limitations (Hindelang *et al.*, 1981; Junger-Tas *et al.*, 1994). Firstly, respondents may conceal or exaggerate offending (Mayhew and Elliott, 1990: 91). So, for example, some may be overly eager to satisfy the perceived needs of the interviewer to hear about offending, whilst others may be reluctant to reveal their offending to interviewers through lack of trust that their responses will be treated confidentially. Whilst the interviewers felt that the presence of others only influenced respondents in five per cent of cases, it is still possible that such a presence affected respondents. Furthermore, as with all surveys which attempt to elicit information retrospectively, factual and temporal distortions can occur as a consequence of recall or memory problems. American research on self-report offending by young people suggests that a substantial minority of respondents have difficulty remembering the answers to some questions (Marshall and Webb, 1994).

One way to validate responses is to check them against official records. However, it was decided from the outset that in order to maximise the response rate, it would be necessary to ensure that respondents are fully satisfied that any information they offer is treated in strict confidence. To this end, they were given an assurance that any offences they revealed to interviewers would be recorded anonymously. This assurance would have been compromised had the interviewers also asked respondents for their permission to check their responses against official records. Interviewing others, such as teachers and parents, can also help to improve the validity of survey data, but due to resource constraints this was not possible. This meant, however, that there was no way of knowing the full extent to which respondents may have concealed (or indeed exaggerated) their offending behaviour. However Farrington (1989) has demonstrated that self-reported offending predicts future convictions among those who have not yet been convicted, which is a relatively convincing demonstration of the validity of the self-report method. An assessment of the validity issue by Marshall and Webb (1992) also concluded that the self-report method represented a reasonably valid measure of crime, although they suggest that studies based on self-report data tend to undersample serious offenders and underestimate the prevalence and frequency of offending among the population under scrutiny.

A second limitation of the self-report method is that individuals for whom self-reports are not obtained – as a result of non response, non-completion or exclusion from the sampling frame – are more likely than average to be those who are engaged in serious or frequent offending or those with characteristics associated with an increased risk of offending (Rutter and Giller 1983). Although the overall response rate of 69 per cent is about average for a survey of this kind, those who did not respond may be disproportionately involved in offending.

Thirdly, self-report surveys only question a sample of the population and sampling error may consequently occur. Estimates are likely to be imprecise, particularly for infrequent offences. Although sampling from pre-selected addresses ensures that interviewers have no choice over who to interview (which ensures the sample is as random as possible), non-respondents were found to be more likely than respondents to live in poorly maintained dwellings and run down neighbourhoods. The sample is therefore slightly biased towards respondents living in better accommodation (see Appendix A).

Finally, it is suggested that because household surveys exclude those living in institutions, such as residential homes, hospitals, prisons and student accommodation, as well as the homeless, they may be unrepresentative. Notwithstanding the complexities of sampling institutional populations, rough estimates of the number of young people aged 14 to 25 who are homeless or living in institutions suggested that even if they had been included in the random selection process, their number would have been less than one per cent of the overall sample.

Notwithstanding these limitations, the self-report method overcomes the main difficulties which are encountered when measuring crime using official records. Given the relatively low rate of detection for many crimes, official data can only give a partial and biased picture of the crime problem. Self-report data allows some low level estimate of the prevalence and incidence of offending to be calculated, enables the characteristics of offenders to be examined and, together with data from victim surveys, can illuminate the so-called dark figure of crime.

Life history research

Life-history interviews were used to explore in depth the processes leading to desistance. A small sub-sample of young people (10 males and 11 females) were identified from the survey as desisters and interviewed retrospectively about their offending 'career' and how changes in their personal circumstances influenced the frequency of their offending and ultimately their desistance from offending. A semi-structured interview schedule was designed on the basis of a small number of pilot interviews. The interviews explored the mechanisms which trigger desistance from offending and how specific life events actually exert their effects. They focused on changes in relationships with family members and friends, the establishment of new family ties, acquiring stable employment and housing, and changing leisure patterns (including the consumption of drugs and alcohol).

The findings from the life-history interviews are akin to case studies and cannot be generalised to the overall population of young offenders or desisters. The interviews constitute subjective accounts of the lives of a small group of individuals and should only be seen as a supplement to the survey findings. They cannot fully explain desistance, but they can help to illuminate some of the processes which lead to desistance.

Structure of the report

Chapter 2 covers the extent and nature of offending among young people. It shows how many young people commit offences, how many offences they commit and how these participation and frequency rates vary by sex and ethnic origin. Chapter 3 describes when offending starts and how patterns of offending change with age. Chapter 4 examines the relationship between an individual's likelihood of starting to offend and a range of factors, such as their family background, school experiences and friendships. Chapter 5 describes the rate at which young men and women make the transition from childhood to adulthood and explains desistance from offending in terms of the "landmarks" passed in moving towards mature adulthood. Chapter 6 presents the findings from the life-history interviews, exploring in greater depth the reasons why some young men and young women stop offending while others do not. Chapter 7 draws conclusions and sets out the implications of the study for the development of policy.

2 Patterns of offending

This chapter describes the extent and nature of criminal offending by 14- to 25- year olds. Some data on patterns of offending by 14- to 21- year olds has been presented elsewhere (Bowling, Graham and Ross, 1994), but this chapter extends the age range and includes a more detailed presentation of how patterns vary by sex and ethnic origin. It also describes patterns of participation and frequency of drug use by 14- to 25- year olds, again broken down by gender and ethnicity.

Participation in offending

The extent of crime may be measured in a number of ways using offender-based data (Tarling, 1993). *Participation* in offending is a measure of the proportion of the population that has committed an offence (equivalent to those cautioned or convicted of an offence in official records). This may be separated into *cumulative participation* – the proportion of the population who committed an offence at any time prior to the survey *(ever offenders)* and *current participation* – the proportion of the population who committed an offence in 1992 *(active offenders)*.

For the purposes of this chapter, an "offender" is defined as somebody who admits committing any one from a list of 23 criminal offences (see Appendix B). These offences are categorised into three offence groups – acquisitive property (e.g. theft, burglary), expressive property (vandalism and arson) and violence (e.g. assault, robbery) – which are then combined into an *overall offences* category. Drug offences are presented separately because the extent of participation is considerably greater than any other form of offending, and the patterns and frequency of use are rather different from those of property and violent offences.[1]

Property and violent offending

Table 2.1 shows that 55 per cent of males (n=404) and 31 per cent of females (n=313) aged between 14 and 25 admitted committing at least one

---

1   Information on other offences – in particular fare dodging and motoring offences – was also collected but the findings are not presented here. See Bowling, Graham and Ross (1994) for a description of these offences among 14- to 21- year olds.

of these 23 criminal offences at some time in their lives, while 28 per cent of males and 12 per cent of females admitted committing an offence during 1992. Just under one-half of males and just over one-quarter of females admitted committing a property offence ever, while 22 per cent and nine per cent, respectively, admitted doing so during 1992. Twenty-eight per cent of males and 10 per cent of females admitted ever committing an act of violence against the person, while nine per cent and four per cent, respectively, admitted doing so in the previous year. Similarly, 25 per cent of males and 16 per cent of females admitted to having ever damaged property in some way or another (i.e. vandalism or arson), while six per cent and four per cent respectively did so in the previous year.

Table 2.1
Cumulative and current participation in offending by sex

Offence group ↓	Cumulative participation					Current participation				
	all ↓	females males ↓		ratio ↓	s.s[1] ↓	all	males ↓	females	ratio ↓	s.s
	%	%	%	%	%	%	%	%	%	%
Property	39	49	28	2.5	****	16	22	9	2.8	****
Violence	19	28	10	3.5	****	7	9	4	2.3	***
Expressive	21	25	16	1.7	****	5	6	4	1.7	*
All offences†	43	55	31	2.7	****	20	28	12	2.3	****
Unweighted N‡	1,648	738	910			1,538	676	862		

Core sample, weighted percentages
† Excluding drug offences
1 Statistical significance (* p<0.05; ** p<0.01; *** p<0.001; **** p<0.0001)
‡ Excludes non-respondents

A number of individual offences were admitted by a significant proportion of the sample (see Table C1 in Appendix C). Among males, five offences were committed "ever" by at least 10 per cent of the sample – vandalism, shoplifting, theft from work, handling stolen goods and fighting. Among females, two offences – shoplifting and handling stolen goods – had been committed at some time by at least 10 per cent of the sample. Among the offences of violence against the person, fighting and disorder was the most prevalent (24 per cent males and eight per cent females) while serious assault (eight per cent males and one per cent females) and wounding (seven per cent males and two per cent females) were relatively rare.[2]

---

2 Fighting consists of those who "participated in fighting or disorder in a group in a public place (for example, football ground, railway station, music festival, riot, demonstration, or just in the streets). Serious assault comprises those who had "beaten up someone not belonging to their immediate family, to such an extent that they thought or knew that medical help or a doctor was needed". Wounding comprised those who had "hurt someone with a knife, stick or other weapon".

The four most prevalent offences committed during 1992 were the same among males and females (see Table C2 in Appendix C). The most common offences were buying and selling stolen goods (males 13 per cent, females seven per cent), fighting (males seven per cent, females three per cent), shoplifting (males five per cent, females two per cent) and vandalism (males four per cent, females two per cent).

Drug use

Drug use is widespread among this age group. Nearly half of the males (45 per cent) and more than one-quarter of the females (26 per cent) had, at some time, used controlled drugs (see Table 2.2). The most common were cannabis (41 per cent of males and 25 per cent of females), LSD (11 per cent of males, seven per cent of females), amphetamines (13 per cent of males and 6 per cent of females), magic mushrooms (12 per cent males and four per cent females) and ecstasy (nine per cent males and five per cent females). Only a small minority had ever tried cocaine (three per cent males and two per cent females), crack (two per cent males and one per cent females) and heroin (two per cent males and less than one per cent females). The British Crime Survey (BCS) found somewhat lower levels of drug use amongst 14- to 25- year olds in 1991, one year earlier (Mott and Mirrlees-Black, 1995). According to the BCS, 30 per cent of males and 23 per cent of females had ever used controlled drugs. Cannabis was the most commonly used drug (24 per cent of males and 19 per cent of females).

About one-fifth of respondents reported using controlled drugs in the last year (29 per cent males and 15 per cent females). The drugs most often used in 1992 reflect the pattern of those taken ever and, as illustrated above, most drug use is confined to the consumption of cannabis.

Sex differences in participation in offending and drug use

As Table 2.1 shows, males were about two and a half times as likely as females to have ever offended or to have offended in the year prior to the survey. The ratio between male and female rates of participation in offending increases with the seriousness of the offence. Taking cumulative participation, the male-female ratio is less than 2:1 for expressive property offences, 2.5:1 for acquisitive property offences and 3.5:1 for violent offences. Tables C1 and C2 in Appendix C show the ratio between male and female offending for individual offences committed ever and last year, respectively. Theft from and of cars and burglary, for example, are, respectively, four, six and eight times more common among males than females. Similarly males are over-represented by a factor of over eight in theft from work and by a factor of nearly seven in fraud. Males are about twice as likely as females to ever use drugs, but approximately five times as likely as females ever to have used heroin (see Table 2.2).

Table 2.2
Cumulative and current participation in drug use, by sex

Drug	Cumulative participation					Current participation				
	all ↓	males females ↓	↓	ratio ↓	s.s¹ ↓	all	males ↓ females	↓	ratio	s.s
	%	%	%	%	%	%	%	%	%	%
Cannabis	33	41	25	2	****	22	29	15	2	****
Heroin	1	2	<1	5	**	<1	<1	<1	<1	
Methadone	2	2	1	2	**	1	1	1	2	
Cocaine	2	3	2	2	**	1	1	1	1	
Crack	1	2	1	2	*	1	1	1	2	
Ecstasy	7	9	5	2	***	4	5	3	2	
Acid/LSD	9	11	7	2	**	5	7	3	2	**
Tranquillizers	1	1	1	2	*	1	1	<1	3	
Amphetamines	9	13	6	2	****	5	7	4	2	*
Temazepam	1	1	1	1		1	<1	1	<1	
Angel Dust	<1	<1	<1	2	*	<1	0	<1	<1	
Magic Mushroom	8	12	4	3	****	3	4	1	4	***
Glue/Gas	4	5	3	1		1	2	1	3	*
Any drug	36	45	26	2	****	24	32	17	2	****
Unweighted N	1,659	745	914			1,659	745	914		

Core sample, weighted percentages
1 Statistical significance: * p<0.05; ** p<0.01; *** p<0.001; **** p<0.0001

Ethnic differences in participation in offending and drug use

Table 2.3 shows the proportion of each ethnic group who admitted ever committing an offence based on the entire sample (i.e. including the ethnic minority booster sample). These data indicate that, taking all offences together, white and Afro-Caribbean respondents have very similar rates of participation in offending (44 per cent and 43 per cent, respectively), while each of the Asian groups have substantially lower rates of participation in offending – Indians 30 per cent, Pakistanis 28 per cent and Bangladeshis 13 per cent.

Table 2.3
Cumulative participation in offending by ethnic origin

Offence group	White	Black	Indian	Pakistani	Bangladeshi
	%	%	%	%	%
Property offences	39	38	25****	24****	12****
Violent offences	19	25	13	18	7***
Expressive offences	22	21	12***	16***	7***
All offences†	44	43	30****	28****	13****
Unweighted N	1,500	202	208	205	104

All samples (including booster sample); weighted percentages.
† Excluding drug offences
* p<0.05; ** p<0.01; *** p<0.001; **** p<0.0001.
"Other Asian" and "other" ethnic groups were excluded from this analysis.

This pattern of ethnic differences in participation in offending is broadly consistent for acquisitive and expressive property offences and for violence. It is evident from these data that although the overall picture is confirmed (i.e. similar rates of offending among Afro-Caribbeans and whites, and substantially lower offending among Asians) there is a wide range of variation in the types of offences committed by each ethnic group. Comparing participation rates for individual offences among different ethnic groups by gender is limited by the small numbers involved for many offences (see Tables C3 and C4 in Appendix C), but there are some significant differences. Amongst males, whites are considerably more likely to be involved in fraud and theft from the workplace, whereas Afro-Caribbeans and Indians are more likely to steal from schools. White and Pakistani males are also significantly more likely to commit acts of vandalism than their Afro-Caribbean, Indian or Bangladeshi counterparts. Amongst females, Afro-Caribbeans are more likely to have ever committed an offence than females from other ethnic groups, particularly Asians, and they are significantly more likely to be involved in stealing from shops, handling stolen goods and fighting.

Table 2.4 shows that respondents from ethnic minority groups, including those of Afro-Caribbean origin, were significantly less likely to have used drugs than white respondents. While 37 per cent of the white young people sampled admitted ever using drugs, 24 per cent of Afro-Caribbeans, 20 per cent of Indians, 14 per cent of Pakistanis and six per cent of Bangladeshis admitted to doing so. Table C5, Appendix C, shows differences in rates of drug use for individual drugs broken down by ethnic origin and sex. Amongst males, whites are significantly more likely to use cannabis and ecstasy than other ethnic groups and, along with Indians, are more likely to use Acid/LSD, Amphetamines and Magic Mushrooms. Amongst females, whites and Afro-Caribbeans are significantly more likely to use cannabis than

Asian females and, as with males, white females are more likely to use Acid/LSD, Amphetamines and Magic Mushrooms than other ethnic groups.

Table 2.4
Cumulative participation in drug use by ethnic origin

Drug	White	Black	Indian	Pakistani	Bangladeshi
	%	%	%	%	%
Cannabis	34	22*	18****	10****	6****
Heroin	1	<1	1	1	0
Methadone	1	3	3	3	1
Cocaine	3	2	1	2	0
Crack	1	2	3	1	0
Ecstasy	8	3	1**	1**	0*
Acid/LSD	10	2*	7**	2**	2*
Tranquillizers	1	<1	1	0	0
Amphetamines	9	<1***	9**	0****	0**
Temazepam	1	0	1	0	0
Angel Dust	<1	0	1	0	0
Magic Mushrooms	8	3**	6**	1***	0**
Glue/Gas	4	1*	<1**	2	0*
Any drug	37	24*	20****	14****	6****
Unweighted N	1,511	204	209	207	106

All samples (including booster sample); weighted percentages
n.s.= non-significant *p<=0.05 **p<0.01 ***p<0.001 ****p<0.0001
"Other Asian" and "other ethnic groups" were excluded from this analysis.

There are at least three possible explanations for the findings on ethnic minority involvement in participation in offending and drug use. Firstly, ethnic minorities may indeed have rates of offending and drug use that are either similar to, or lower than their white counterparts. Other recent self-report studies in The Netherlands, Belgium and Germany have also found similar or lower rates of overall offending among ethnic minorities compared with whites (Junger-Tas et al, 1994). However, caution should be exercised in making direct comparisons with these countries given the different origin and cultural and socio-economic characteristics of their ethnic minority populations.

A higher rate of drug use by whites has also been found by other studies in England and Wales. For example, a report produced for the Home Office

Central Drugs Prevention Unit (Leitner, Shapland and Wiles, 1993) found that considerably more whites aged 16 to 25 admitted to using drugs than Afro-Caribbeans (51 per cent compared with 34 per cent) and nearly five times as many whites admitted using drugs as Asians. The BCS, however, found little differences between whites and Afro-Caribbeans in terms of overall drug use, although three times as many of both groups admitted using drugs as Asians (Mott and Mirrlees-Black, 1995).

Secondly, the sample may be skewed towards a low-offending and low drug-using group of ethnic minorities. Ethnic minority respondents were less likely than other groups to complete the drug use and offending booklets. Non-completion rates were three per cent for whites, eight per cent for blacks and Indians, 15 per cent for Pakistanis and 11 per cent for Bangladeshis. If those who refused or otherwise failed to answer questions on drug use and offending did so because they were unwilling to admit these activities, then the ethnic minority sample will be skewed towards a less delinquent population than the white sample. It is, however, difficult to assess the characteristics of non-respondents and any skew in the sample towards a low offending and drug using group of ethnic minorities will be at least partly offset by the lower overall refusal rate to participate in the survey of ethnic minorities and the skew of the ethnic minority sample towards areas of high ethnic minority concentration, where rates of drug use and offending tend to be higher.

Those with language difficulties (1.4 per cent of total sample, including ethnic booster sample) were also considerably less likely to complete the offending booklet than those without such difficulties, although the Asians were more likely to report language difficulties than whites or Afro-Caribbeans.[3] The non-contact rate for ethnic minorities (as estimated by comparing the response rates in the core and ethnic minority booster samples) was also slightly higher (although no different from the non-contact rate in the high crime sample), but this is probably cancelled out by a lower refusal rate (again as estimated by comparing the refusal rates in the core and booster samples).

Finally, those from ethnic minorities may be more likely to conceal their offending behaviour or conversely, whites may be more likely to exaggerate their offending. In the US, Hindelang et al (1981) found that black males tended to under-report offending behaviour compared with other ethnic groups and whilst some evidence for this exists in other countries (Junger, 1989),[4] there are reasons for resisting the temptation to infer universal

---

3   Respondents who did not complete the booklets because they had difficulty reading English were excluded from this analysis.

4   In the context of low rates of admission of offending and police contact for all ethnic groups, Junger (1989) found lower rates of admission (and therefore lower validity of self-report) among Moroccan and Turkish respondents, but little difference between the responses of Surinamese and indigenous Dutch respondents (see also Bowling, 1990).

lessons from this (Bowling, 1990). To date, however, there is no evidence in the UK on which to base an assessment of the willingness of different ethnic groups to admit offending or drug-taking.

Frequency of offending

An additional measure of the extent of offending is the frequency with which individual offences are committed.[5] Active offenders were asked how often they had offended in the past year (Table 2.5).

Table 2.5
Frequency of offending in previous year (1992) among active offenders only, by sex

Offence group	Males number of offences				Females number of offences			
	1-2	3-5	6-10	11+	1-2	3-5	6-10	11+
	%	%	%	%	%	%	%	%
Property	52	16	18	15	66	25	3	6
Violence	75	18	6	1	86	11	1	3
Expressive	54	26	6	15	33	34	17	13
All offences†	56	17	13	15	57	32	4	7
Unweighted N	100	30	23	27	44	25	3	5

Core sample, weighted percentages
†Excluding drug offences.
Row total may not equal 100 per cent due to rounding

More than half of the offenders – 56 per cent of males and 57 per cent of females – committed only one or two offences in the year prior to the survey, 26 per cent of male offenders and nine per cent of female offenders committed more than five but less than 50 offences, while four males and one female committed more than 50 offences. Of those who committed a violent offence, approximately three out of four males and nearly nine out of 10 females did so only once or twice.

In order to assess the extent to which offending is concentrated amongst a small group of offenders or spread more widely, certain assumptions needed to be made since frequency data was only collected in bands (once, twice,

---

5   Estimates of frequency of offending tend to be less reliable in self-report studies than estimates of participation (Hindelang *et al*, 1981).

3-5 times, 6-10 times, 11-20 times and more than 20 times). On the basis that offenders committed the lowest number of offences in each frequency band and that the maximum number of offences any offender committed is 20, 26 per cent of offences were committed by three per cent of offenders. Clearly this is an underestimate (the three per cent will have committed a higher proportion of offences than 26 per cent), but the figure provides a useful low level baseline. On the same basis, 73 per cent of offences were committed by 22 per cent of offenders (again this will be an underestimate).

Regularity of drug use

The nature of drug use is such that respondents were asked about frequency patterns in a different way from rates for other offences. Rather than asking respondents to estimate the number of individual occasions that they had used drugs, information was recorded on how *regularly* they used them (see Table 2.6).

Table 2.6
Regularity of drug use "last year" (1992) among active drug users, by sex

1. Males

Drug	Once or twice		Once every couple of months		1-3 times a month		1-5 times a week		every day	
	n	%	n	%	n	%	n	%	n	%
Cannabis	71	32	37	17	40	18	61	28	10	5
Other drugs†	47	56	15	18	11	13	11	13	<1	<1

Unweighted N = 219 (cannabis) and 85 (other drugs).

2. Females

Drug	Once or twice		Once every couple of months		1-3 times a month		1-5 times a week		every day	
	n	%	n	%	n	%	n	%	n	%
Cannabis	62	55	11	10	14	13	23	20	3	3
Other drugs†	26	52	4	9	10	20	8	17	1	2

Unweighted N = 113 (cannabis) and 49 (other drugs).
Core sample, weighted percentages
† Heroin, Methadone/Physeptone, Cocaine, Crack, Acid/LSD, Tranquillizers, Amphetamines, Temazepam, Angel Dust/PCP, Ecstasy/MDMA ('E'), Magic Mushrooms, Glue/Gas/Aerosols (to sniff or inhale).

Whilst many cannabis users were relatively infrequent in their use – about one-third (32 per cent) of male and half (55 per cent) of females used it once or twice in the past year – a substantial minority used cannabis at least once a week (33 per cent of males and 22 per cent of females). Similarly, for other controlled drugs, more than half the male (56 per cent) and female (52 per cent) users did so once or twice in the previous year, but 13 per cent of males and 19 per cent of females used one or more of these drugs once a week or more.

Sex differences in frequency of offending

As well as being less likely to ever start offending, active female offenders committed, on average, substantially fewer offences than males (Table 2.7). The overall ratio between male and female frequency of offending was around 2:1, but this changes with offence type. The average number of property offences committed by male offenders is seven compared with three for females (ratio=2.2:1); the average number of violent offences is three for males, two for females (ratio=1.4:1). The male:female ratio for expressive property offences is 1:1. These averages are, however, slight underestimates since frequency counts were calculated on the basis that offenders committed the lowest number of offences in each frequency band and that the maximum number of offences any offender committed is 20.

Table 2.7
Average number of offences committed last year by sex (active offenders only)

Offence group	Males	Females	Sex ratio
Property offences	7	3	2.2
Violent offences	3	2	1.4
Expressive offences	5	5	1.0
All offences †	7	4	1.8
Unweighted 'n'	175	113	

Core sample, weighted data
† Excluding drug offences

Ethnic differences in frequency of offending

Table 2.8 shows the frequency with which offenders of each ethnic origin admitted committing offences in the past year (again, these averages are slight underestimates). It can be seen that the average frequency among white offenders was six offences during 1992 compared with five offences for Afro-Caribbeans, eight for Indians, three for Pakistanis and Bangladeshis. These data, along with the data presented earlier in Table 2.3, indicate that young people from Asian backgrounds tend not only to be less likely than whites and Afro-Caribbeans to start offending but, with the exception of Indians, to offend less frequently if they do start.

Table 2.8
Average number of offences committed last year by ethnic origin (active offenders only)

Offence group	White	Black	Indian	Pakistani/ Bangladeshi‡
Property offences	5	5	8	3
Violent offences	3	3	1	2
Expressive offences	5	1	5	4
All offences	6	5	8	3
Unweighted N	252	26	20	26

All samples (including booster sample), weighted percentages
"Other Asian" and "other ethnic groups" not included as numbers too small
‡ Pakistani and Bangladeshi respondents were combined due to small numbers

Serious offending

A sub-category of *serious offences* was constructed comprising car theft, bag snatching, burglary, robbery, fighting, arson, assault and wounding. Twenty-one per cent of males and five per cent of females ever committed a serious offence, while seven per cent of males and two per cent of females did so during 1992.

For the most serious offences the male:female ratio is just over 5:1 and approximately twice as many Afro-Caribbeans (15 per cent) and whites (13 per cent) are involved in serious offending as Indians (8 per cent), Pakistanis (8 per cent) and Bangladeshis (six per cent). The average number of serious offences committed by males and females were six and two respectively (ratio=3:1).

Summary

The survey findings presented here describe the extent and nature of criminal offences committed by a representative sample of 14- to 25- year olds "ever" and during 1992. The main conclusions of the chapter are:

- About one in two males and one in three females admitted offending at some time in their lives, while around one in four males and one in eight females admitted offending during 1992.

- Just under one in two males and just over one in four females committed a property offence "ever" while one in five and one in ten, respectively, admitted doing so in 1992. About one in three males and one in ten females committed an act of violence against the person ever, while one in ten and one in 20, respectively, admitted doing so in 1992.

- Males are about three times as likely as females to commit a criminal offence, although they are five times more likely to commit a serious offence.

- The majority of offenders commit only one or two offences; about three per cent of offenders are responsible for at least 26 per cent of all offences.

- Just under one in two males and just over one in four females had ever used controlled drugs, while one in three males and one in six females had done so in 1992. The most common were cannabis, LSD, amphetamines, Magic Mushrooms and Ecstasy. Use of heroin, crack and cocaine was rare. Most drug users did so relatively infrequently, but around one in three male and one in five female cannabis users did so once a week or more.

- Black and white respondents had similar rates of participation in offending (about four in ten), while those of Indian (one in four), Pakistani (one in four) and Bangladeshi (one in eight) origin had significantly lower rates than whites. This pattern was broadly consistent across offence types. In general, ethnic minority offenders committed no more offences than whites.

- Ethnic minorities were significantly less likely to have used drugs than whites. While more than one in three whites had ever used drugs, about one in four blacks, one in five Indians, one in seven Pakistanis and one in 17 Bangladeshis had done so.

3 Age and offending

Explaining why some young people start to offend and why some later desist requires information about how patterns of offending change with age. It is necessary to know when offending starts, when the peak rate of participation and frequency is reached, the rate at which offending declines thereafter and whether young people actually desist from offending, or simply switch to offences with a lower risk of detection. This chapter therefore focuses on how rates of participation and levels of frequency in offending and drug use change with age and how these changes differ between males and females.

Age of onset

Discovering *when* offending begins is a prerequisite to explaining *how* it begins (see Chapter 4). The age at which offending starts also has implications for desistance from offending, early starters tending to offend more frequently and to continue offending longer than late starters (Tarling, 1993; Blumstein *et al*, 1986; Farrington, 1992; Rutter and Giller ,1983).[1]

It can be seen from Table 3.1 (see over page) that the peak age of onset (the most popular age at which young people start to offend) is 15 for males and 15 for females.[2] The mean age of onset (the average age at which young people start to offend) for both males and females is about 13.5 (s.d.=3.7). The difference between the peak and mean or average age of onset can be explained by a skew towards the younger end of the age range. In other words, many young people start offending before and during their early teens, so more start to offend before the peak age of offending than after it. Obversely, few young people start to use drugs before the age of 16 (the peak age), whereas many start to use drugs after the age of 16. This is consistent with the findings of longitudinal research which generally shows a peak age of first offence (not first conviction) between 13 and 15 (Farrington, 1994a).

---

1   A longitudinal design, which collects information prospectively, is the most reliable way of estimating age of onset. For practical purposes, however, a cross-sectional design had to be employed in this study, which meant that information on onset of offending had to be collected retrospectively and may therefore be subject to recall error.

2   The mean age of onset will depend to some extent on current age; the older the respondent the more likely he/she will have started to offend later. However, this is not relevant to comparisons of behaviours since they will all be subject to the same minor distortions.

Table 3.1
Age of onset for a range of delinquent behaviours

	Males		Females	
	Mean age of onset	*Peak age of onset*	*Mean age of onset*	*Peak age of onset*
First truancy	13.5	14	13.6	14
First ran away	13.1	14	13.1	14
First drink	13.0	14	13.0	14
First cannabis	16.8	15	16.8	15
First other drugs	17.0	16	17.0	16
First offence†	13.5	15	13.5	15

Core sample, weighted figures
Unweighted n=738 (males); n=910 (females)
† Excluding drug offences

The findings presented in Table 3.1 also indicate that offending starts at about the same time as other forms of delinquent behaviour, during the early to mid-teens. Running away from home, truancy from school, drinking alcohol and offending start, on average, at around 13 for both boys and girls. Drug-taking, however, starts *on average* at least three years later at around 16 for girls and 17 for boys, even though the most common age at which cannabis use and offending start is 15. The fact that the average age of onset for drug use is considerably older than the peak age, whereas the average age of onset for offending is younger than the peak age suggests that most drug users start at or *after* the peak age whereas most offenders start *before* the peak age.

Participation in offending by age and sex

Table 3.2 shows the proportion of the sample within each age group who admitted committing an offence during 1992 by offence group (Table C6, Appendix C shows the same breakdown for each individual criminal offence).[3]

Among males, expressive and violent offences were most prevalent among 14- to 17-year-olds. Property offences, excluding fraud and theft from work, were most prevalent among 18- to 21-year-olds, although the theft of motor vehicles is most prevalent amongst 22- to 25-year-olds (see Table C6, Appendix C). If fraud and theft from work are included (which increase dramatically during the early twenties), 22- to 25-year-olds have the highest rate of offending. The

---

3   It should be remembered that this is a cross-sectional (rather than longitudinal) sample so it not possible to distin-
     guish the effect of chronological age from the effect of generational change. This means that the rate of offending
     among those in the 14-17 cohort may not be identical to the rate of offending by this cohort when they reach 18-21
     or indeed 22-25.

proportion of current male offenders aged 22 to 25 who admitted to theft from the workplace is nearly three times the number of 18- to 21-year-olds, which is likely, at least in part, to reflect the increase in opportunities for committing such offences as more young men take on employment. Fraud increases even more dramatically and is the most prevalent offence amongst 22- to 25-year-old males. Nearly one in seven young men aged 22 to 25 admitted to committing at least one act of fraud in the year prior to the survey (see Table C6, Appendix C). Taking all offences together, participation increases from around one in four male juveniles (14-17) to just under one in three young male adults (18-25). For females, taking all offences together, offending is most prevalent among juveniles. Around one in five 14- to 17-year-olds offended, compared with one in ten 18- to 21-year-olds and less than one in twenty-five 22- to 25-year-olds.

Table 3.2
Current participation in offending by age group and sex

Offence group	Males				Females			
	14-17	18-21	22-25	s.s.[1]	14-17	18-21	22-25	s.s.
	%	%	%	%	%	%	%	%
Property offences	17	25	27	*	13	9	3	**
Violent offences	12	9	4	**	7	4	<1	**
Expressive offences	8	8	0	***	8	1	<1	****
All offences†	24	31	31		19	11	4	****
Unweighted N	276	227	173		303	284	275	

Core sample, weighted percentages
† Excluding drug offences
1 Statistical significance: * p<0.05; ** p<0.01; *** p<0.001; **** p<0.0001

These findings indicate that, among males, the rate of participation in offending does not change dramatically between the ages of 14 and 25, but it does change markedly in character. Expressive behaviour directed against property – such as vandalism and arson – is most common in the mid-teens but all but ceases by the early twenties. Violent behaviour – ranging in seriousness from fighting to wounding – increases during the teenage years then drops off sharply in the twenties. Property offending remains relatively constant throughout this period, but as the most visible forms (such as shoplifting and burglary) decrease during the early twenties, less detectable forms of offending such as fraud and theft from work start to increase. Although most of those starting to commit fraud and theft from work during their late teens had switched from other offences, about 30 per cent were new offenders. For females, with the exception of drug offences, the prevalence of offending of all types drops off sharply after the mid-teens.

Drug use

Table 3.3 shows the proportion of the sample within each age group who admitted using drugs in the previous year.

Table 3.3
Current drug use, by age and sex

Offence group	Males				Females			
	All	14-17	18-21	22-25	All	14-17	18-21	22-25
	%	%	%	%	%	%	%	%
Cannabis	29	14	45	28****	15	16	20	5****
Heroin	<1	<1	1	0	<1	0	1	<1
Methadone	1	1	2	<1	1	1	1	1
Cocaine	1	0	1	3**	1	0	2	1
Crack	1	<1	1	2**	1	1	1	0
Ecstasy	5	2	8	5**	3	3	6	<1**
Acid/LSD	7	5	11	4*	3	4	5	1
Tranquillizers	1	1	3	<1	<1	<1	<1	1
Amphetamines	7	2	9	10**	4	3	7	2**
Temazepam	<1	<1	1	1	1	1	3	0 *
Angel Dust	0	0	0	0	<1	0	<1	0
Mushrooms	4	3	7	2*	1	1	1	1
Glue/Gas	2	1	4	<1	1	1	1	0
Any drug	32	17	47	31****	17	17	22	8***
Unweighted N	745	308	244	193	914	324	305	285

Core sample, weighted percentages
*p<0.05 **p <0.01 ***p <0.001 ****p <0.0001

Drug use was most prevalent in the 18 to 21 age group, among which nearly half of males (47%) and more than one-fifth of females (22%) had used drugs in the previous year. While drug use was far more prevalent among males than females among those aged 18 or over, roughly the same proportion of males and females admitted using drugs among those aged 14 to 17. The British Crime Survey found a slightly higher rate of ever drug use for 14- to 17-year-old males (22%), but a lower rate for 18- to 21-year-old males (37%) (Mott and Mirrlees-Black).[4]

---

[4]   It may be that the greater reluctance on the part of the younger respondents in this survey to admit to using drugs than in the British Crime Survey is related to the presence of others at the interview stage (see Appendix A). Younger members are more likely to have had someone present at the interview and may have been inhibited from admitting to using drugs under such circumstances.

Peak age of offending and drug use

Table 3.4 shows the "peak" age of offending across the 14 to 25 age range for different offence groups. (The peak age of offending differs from the peak age of onset in that the former depicts the age at which most offenders start to offend whereas the latter comprises the age at which the rate of participation in offending is at its highest.)

Table 3.4
Mean and peak age of offending

	Males			Females		
	Mean	Peak	S.D.	Mean	Peak	S.D.
Property offences	19.6	20	3.2	17.3	15	2.6
Property offences†	18.6	20	2.9	17.3	15	2.6
Violent offences	17.9	16	3.0	17.0	16	2.1
Expressive offences	17.3	14	2.4	15.9	15	1.5
All offences ‡	19.4	21	3.3	17.2	16	2.5
Drug offences	19.9	20	2.6	18.5	17	2.7

Core sample, weighted figures

† excluding theft from the workplace and fraud

‡ excluding drug offences

S.D. = standard deviation from the mean

Among males, the peak age of offending is 14 for expressive property offences, 16 for violent offences, 17 for serious offences and 20 for drug and acquisitive property offences. Among females, the peak age of offending is 15 for property, expressive and serious offences, 16 for violent offences and 17 for drug offences.

Table 3.4 also shows the mean age of male and female offenders within the 14 to 25 age range. As with the peak age, the average age of male offenders tends to be older than for females. For females, the peak age of offending (including drug use) is lower than the mean age. This means that more females offend after the peak age than before. For males, however, the opposite is true, but only because of the predominance of property offending by younger males. However, it should be noted that rather than offending reaching a sharp peak within any one age group, it increases and decreases only gently at either side of these maxima, as reflected in the relatively large standard deviations from the mean.

The ratio of offending between males and females

Earlier it was shown that the male:female offending ratio increased with the seriousness of the offence; Table 3.5 shows that the magnitude of the male:female sex ratio also increases with age. For example, while the sex-ratios for acquisitive property offences and for violent offences are around 1:1 among 14- to 17-year-olds, these rise to around 3:1 among 18- to 21-year-olds and over 10:1 among 22- to 25-year-olds. Taking all offences together, the male:female ratio rises from just 1.4:1 at age 14 to 17 to 4:1 at 18 to 21 and 11:1 at 22 to 25 years old.

Table 3.5
Male:female ratio of offending, by age

	14–17	18–21	22–25
Property offences	1.3	3.3****	10.3****
Violent offences	1.8 *	2.7**	11.7*
Expressive offences	1.0	7.6***	–
All offences †	1.4	3.7****	11.1****

Core sample, weighted percentages
* p<.05; **p<.0.01; ***p<0.001; ****p<0.0001;
† excluding drug offences

Frequency of offending by age and sex

Table 3.6 shows the average frequency of offending (excluding drug use) among active offenders only, taking account of changes in rates of participation with age. For males, offending tends to decline in frequency for all types of offence after the mid-teens. For females, expressive offences decline after the mid-teens, then remain fairly constant thereafter.

Taking all offences together, active male offenders aged 14 to 17 admitted an average of 11 offences during 1992, 18- to 21-year-olds admitted seven offences and 22- 25-year-olds admitted four offences. For active female offenders, the average number of offences committed in each age group was five, two and three, respectively.

Table 3.6
Average frequency of last year offending by age-group and sex
(active offenders only)

Offence group	Males				Females			
	All	14-17	18-21	22-25	All	14-17	18-21	22-25
	%	%	%	%	%	%	%	%
Property	7	11	6	4	3	4	2	3
Violence	3	3	3	1	2	2	1	2
Expressive	5	9	1	0	5	6	2	0
All offences†	7	11	7	4	4	5	2	3

Core sample, weighted percentages.
†Excluding drug offences

Summary and discussion

The main findings on age and offending and in particular on how participation in, and frequency of offending varies with age and sex during the transition from childhood to adulthood are:

- Offending is most likely to start at the age of 15 for both males and females, around one year later than other forms of problematic behaviour such as running away from home, truancy from school and drinking alcohol. Drug-taking is most likely to start a year later at the age of 16.

- Among males, the peak age of offending is 14 for expressive property offences, 16 for violent offences, 17 for serious offences, 20 for acquisitive property offences and for drug use. Among females, the peak age of offending is 15 for property, expressive and serious offences, 16 for violent offences and 17 for drug use.

- Participation in offending by females declines with age whereas for males this does not appear to be the case. As they grow older, males (as well as females) are much less likely to engage in violent offences, but participation in property offending by males *increases* with age. However, both male and female offenders commit fewer offences after the teenage years.

- Participation in drug use is highest amongst 18- to 21-year-olds, among whom about one in two males and one in five females had taken a drug in 1992.

These findings suggest that the notion that young people "grow out of crime" is an oversimplification, at least for young males. Drug offending apart, girls clearly do grow out of crime when they reach their late teens. But a striking finding is that the prevalence of property crime by males increases with age and that the overall offending rate (excluding drug use) for males increases and then remains constant throughout the 18 to 25 age range. These findings contrast with information on recorded convictions, which show a decline in prevalence rates by males after the age of 18. The increase in the prevalence of property crime may in part be explained by men switching from relatively visible and risky forms of property crime, such as burglary and shoplifting, to less visible, less risky and less detectable forms of property offending, such as fraud and theft from the workplace. Longitudinal studies using official data have also found that as offenders get older, they tend to switch to different offences (Farrington, 1986). However, involvement in expressive property offences, violence and other serious offences do decrease among males during the early twenties, suggesting that offending among most young adults is less publicly visible and also less serious than that of their younger teenage counterparts. It is also the case that while the proportion of the male population which is actively offending does not decline during young adulthood, the frequency with which they commit offences declines substantially. This means that as male offenders grow older, their offending tends to decelerate. Thus, the present study suggests that the decline in recorded convictions after the age of 18 may be due to the majority of young adult male offenders desisting from more visible forms of offending (i.e. those offences with relatively high detection rates) and reducing the frequency at which they offend.

4 Initiating offending: why do some young people start to offend?

Chapters 2 and 3 described the differential involvement in different types of offending by young people aged 14 to 25. This chapter and the next chapter move from a description of patterns of offending towards attempting to explain firstly why some young people start to offend and secondly why some young offenders desist from offending whilst others do not.

In the last chapter it was shown that most young people start to offend during their early teens (see Table 3.1). Therefore, in order to explain why some young people start to offend (and conversely why others do not) it is necessary to examine the influences on young people's lives during and prior to this period of their development. The approach adopted in this study was to compare offenders with non-offenders in terms of their social and demographic backgrounds and their experiences at home and at school. In order that these comparisons could be made – irrespective of the age of the respondent – the sections of the survey questionnaire relating to the onset of offending focused specifically on respondents' lives at the age of 14 to 15. To this end, those aged 14 and 15 were asked questions about their current situation, whilst those aged over 15 were asked to provide the same information retrospectively.[1]

Since the survey is cross sectional – that is it asks questions at only one moment in time – it cannot determine the *causes* of crime (or the *causes* of desistance). The extent to which temporal ordering can be inferred from cross sectional data is limited, although even with longitudinal designs, establishing causal ordering is problematic. However, this study does ascertain which background factors are closely associated with offending (and desistance from offending) and which are not and by posing some questions retrospectively, and establishing the age at which particular events occurred for the first time, it is able to infer temporal ordering in a limited way.

It should also be pointed out that not all the proximal and distal factors which may influence offending behaviour have been included in this analysis. No genetic or biological data were collected and neither were data collected on the individual personalities of respondents. However, it is known from other research that social and demographic variables are the

---

1   Clearly the older the respondent, the more likely they may have problems accurately recalling the circumstances of their lives at the age of 15.

most influential antecedents of criminality (see, for example, Rutter and Giller, 1983; Tarling, 1993; Farrington, 1994a) and of course individual personalities are at least to some extent shaped by and reflected in these background factors.

Other factors which might be correlates of offending, but could not logically, or did not empirically precede the *onset* of offending, are not included in this analysis. Thus, although variables such as forming stable relationships with the opposite sex, starting full time employment or other aspects of the respondents' *current* situation may be correlated with offending, they are unlikely to explain why some young people *start* to offend. A minority of late starters may have been influenced by these other variables, but because the majority of offenders started to offend in their early teens – three-quarters of the sample committed their first offence before the age of 16 – these events are unlikely to have influenced onset at the aggregate level.

The main factors explored here therefore consist of the respondent's social class, family background, family size, structure and relationships, parental supervision, sibling involvement with the police, school experience (attachment to school, standard of school work, attendance) and association with delinquent peers.

There are a number of ways in which the inter-relationships between these factors and offending can be ascertained. The approach adopted here was to firstly explore the bivariate associations between starting to offend and family (including social class), school and peer group variables and secondly construct a model incorporating the strongest variables in order to explore their relative importance. This second stage is essential since an apparent bivariate association between any socio-demographic variable and offending may be less marked (or indeed disappear altogether) when other factors are taken into account.

Defining an "offender" for the purposes of explanatory analysis

In many self-report studies an "offender" is defined as someone who admits any one of a long list of offences (see, for example, Junger-Tas *et al*, 1994). Some of these offenders may only have committed one or two petty crimes and will be virtually indistinguishable from non-offenders. Since the primary purpose of this study is to explain how offenders (and those who desist from offending) are different from non-offenders, a more rigorous definition of an offender was used. Thus in order that respondents could be said to have started to offend, they were categorised as an "ever offender" if they admitted at least three offences from the list of 23 offences or one serious offence from the list (see Appendix B).

Of the total sample of 1,721, 73 failed to answer the question on whether they had ever offended leaving a total usable sample of 1,648. Of these, 57 per cent (334 males and 597 females) said that they had committed none of the core list of offences during the previous year and were defined as "non offenders" while 30 per cent (298 males and 204 females) met the criteria outlined above and were defined as "offenders" for the purpose of this analysis. The remaining 13 per cent (106 males and 109 females) who admitted only one or two minor offences were excluded from the analysis.

Family background and starting to offend

Numerous studies in different countries conducted over a considerable period of time have identified a range of family influences on delinquency (Wadsworth, 1979; West, 1982; Kolvin et al, 1990). These family influences include social class, parental neglect, lack of supervision, poor discipline and control, family discord and separation and parental criminality.[2] In this survey, respondents were asked about their social class background, the size and composition of their family, the quality of their relationships with their parents, how well supervised they thought they were at the age of 14 to 15 and whether they knew whether any of their siblings had been in trouble with the police for committing a criminal offence (see Table 4.1 over page).

Social class

The measure of social class used in this study was based on a standard classification of occupational groups. In most cases this assessment of social class was based on the occupation of the respondent's father, or if this data was unavailable, the occupation of the respondent's mother. If this information was unavailable, the occupation of the respondent was used if they were in employment, which reduced the number of missing cases to a minimum.

Among males, rates of offending were not significantly different between higher and lower socio-economic groups, indicating no class difference in the likelihood of starting to offend. Among females, offending was significantly more common among those from lower socio-economic groups, indicating a relatively strong relationship between social class and offending. It will be seen later in this chapter, however, that the effect of social class disappears once other family factors are taken into account.

---

2 See Utting et al (1993) for a review of the findings of research on families and crime.

Table 4.1
Family factors and offending

Family factor	males offended %	males offended (n)	females offended %	females offended (n)
Socio-economic group	n.s.		***	
I/II	42	(130)	13	(175)
IIINM	38	(67)	15	(80)
IIIM	52	(238)	21	(278)
I V/V	50	(162)	32	(221)
Family structure	*		**	
both natural parents	42	(413)	17	(502)
single parent	49	(100)	23	(150)
natural parent +step parent	57	(51)	36	(50)
Family size	n.s.		n.s.	
no siblings	18	(129)	20	(171)
1 sibling	46	(296)	21	(392)
2 siblings	22	(123)	16	(178)
3 or more siblings	14	(82)	29	
Attachment to family	****		****	
strong	42	(498)	17	(584)
medium/weak	70	(134)	33	(217)
Parental supervision	****		****	
high	32	(201)	14	(410)
medium/low	53	(397)	30	(367)
Siblings in trouble with the police **			****	
siblings in trouble	68	(62)	55	(92)
no siblings in trouble	46	(570)	17	(709)

weighted percentages, unweighted ns.
n.s.=non-significant *p<.05 **p<.0.01 ***p<0.001 ****p<0.0001

These findings are consistent with other self-report studies, many of which have found no association between social class and offending (see, for example, Riley and Shaw, 1985) or only a weak association (see, for example, Rutter and Giller, 1983). This contrasts with findings from studies on recorded convictions or convicted offenders where a strong social class effect is discernible (see, for example, Douglas *et al.*, 1966 and Walmsley *et al.*, 1990 respectively). There are a number of possible explanations for this discrepancy.

One explanation is that the two measures of offending actually measure different things. Self-report studies count "primary offenders", or initial rule breakers, whereas studies using official data count "secondary offenders", or those who have been arrested, prosecuted, convicted and in some cases incarcerated as a consequence of their offending. The effects of social class are stronger for more serious offences (Elliott and Ageton, 1980) and self-report studies tend to include some offences which do not lead to conviction. A separate analysis was conducted which excluded all but the most serious offences; this showed, as expected, a strong relationship with social class for both males and females.

An alternative explanation is that the findings of self-report studies are influenced by class differences in the propensity of respondents to conceal or exaggerate their offending behaviour. Respondents more accustomed to completing questionnaires (i.e. those in higher social classes) may provide a fuller and more detailed account of their offending behaviour (an "education effect"), whilst those who have little or no experience of crime may report more trivial acts than those for whom crime is more commonplace (a "threshold effect").

Family structure

About three-quarters of both males and females in the sample were living with both natural parents at age 14 to 15, 17 per cent of females and 14 per cent of males lived in single parent families and five per cent of females and 19 per cent of males lived with one natural parent and one step-parent. Eleven per cent had other family arrangements, such as living with grandparents, siblings, or two step-parents, or failed to answer this question.

For both males and females, those who lived with both natural parents were the least likely ever to start to offend (males 42 per cent, females 17 per cent), followed by those living with a lone parent (males 49 per cent, females 23 per cent), while those living with one natural and one step-parent were the most likely to start offending (males 57 per cent, females 36 per cent). The difference in offending rates between those brought up by two natural parents and both those brought up in single-parent and step-families was statistically significant for both males and females. However, as illustrated below, once the quality of relationships with parents and their capacity and willingness to supervise their children are taken into account, the influence of family structure disappears. This is consistent with other research which shows that step-families and single-parent-families are not in themselves criminogenic (Utting *et al* 1993; Loeber and Stouthamer-Loeber, 1986).

Family size

About half of both male and female respondents lived in families with one brother or sister when they were 14 to 15, just under one-quarter lived with two siblings, 12 per cent lived with three siblings or more and 18 per cent had no siblings.

Females who grew up in large families (with three or more siblings) had slightly higher rates of offending (41 per cent) than those who grew up in small families (32 per cent), but this finding is only statistically significant at the ten per cent level. Among males, the equivalent figures were 47 per cent and 49 per cent respectively, which are not significantly different.

These findings are somewhat at variance with other research (Wadsworth, 1979; West, 1982) but, as with social class, an effect for family size is more likely to be found in studies using recorded convictions rather than self-report data. In the Cambridge Study of Delinquent Development, no relationship was found between family size and self-report offending among those who had not also been convicted of a criminal offence. Others have suggested that the effects of family size on delinquency are due to the greater levels of stress and poverty experienced by large families (Graham, 1989; Utting *et al*, 1993) and their ability to supervise and control their offspring compared with parents in smaller families (Wilson, 1980).

Attachment to family

Hirschi (1969) has developed a theory of crime causation based on social control. An important component of social control theory is attachment to significant others and he argues that attachment to family members is an important source of protection from deviant behaviour. Two aspects of attachment to the respondent's family of origin were examined in this study – relationships with their parents and running away from home. Those who said that they got on badly with one or other of their parents or, before their 16th birthday, had stayed away from home for at least one night without their parents' knowledge, were defined as having a weak bond with their family.

Using this definition, 21 per cent of both males and females were found to have a weak attachment to their family. Relating this to offending, it can be seen from Table 4.1 that of those who said they were strongly attached to their families, 42 per cent were offenders, whereas of those who said they were weakly or moderately attached to their families, 70 per cent were offenders. Similarly, a higher proportion (twice as many) of female offenders reported weak or moderate attachment to their families. Given the importance of family attachment in explaining delinquency (see, for example, Junger-Tas, 1988) it is worth looking in more detail at which family attachment factors are most closely associated with offending.

Most young people reported getting on well with their parents when they were aged 14 or 15. More than 90 per cent of both males and females said they got on very or fairly well with their mother, while only eight per cent of males and nine per cent of females said that they got on fairly or very badly with her. Less than two per cent said they had no mother or never saw her. Relationships with fathers were not as good; 80 per cent of respondents said they got on fairly or very well with their father while just under 10 per cent said they got on fairly or very badly with him. About 10 per cent said they no longer had a father or never saw him.

Taking only those who had a mother or father at age 14 or 15, those who had a bad relationship with one or other of them were much more likely to admit committing a criminal offence than those who had a good relationship with them. Among females, a third of those who got on badly with their father had offended compared with a sixth of those who got on well with him (p<0.5). Similarly, a third of those who got on badly with their mother had offended compared with a fifth of those who got on well with her (significant only at the 10 per cent level).

Among males, 80 per cent of those who got on badly with their fathers had offended compared with 43 per cent of those who got on well with him (p<0.0001). Similarly, 73 per cent of those who got on badly with their mother had offended compared with 45 per cent of those who got on well with her (p<0.05). It is evident that a bad relationship with a father has a strong and statistically significant relationship with offending for both males and females, particularly for males, while a bad relationship with the mother, although less important, is also related to offending.

Johnson (1987) arrived at the same conclusion in his study of American high school students and Junger-Tas (1993), in assessing the impact of changes in the family on delinquency, also concluded that the role of the father would seem to be critical in determining the offending behaviour of children. But caution should be exercised when drawing causal inferences from this data. It might be that having a bad relationship with a parent has, in itself, a criminogenic effect.

However, it may also be that offending sours the relationship with parents or that a bad relationship has some other effect, such as reducing the capacity of parents to exercise effective supervision (see Gove and Crutchfield, 1982).[3]

When respondents were asked whether they had ever stayed away from home for at least one night without their parents' permission, about seven per cent of both males and females said that they had. Of those who had run away from home, nearly half of the females (46 per cent) and three-quarters of the males (71 per cent) admitted to offending.

The reasons why young people run away from home vary, but include problems at school, rejection from the home, flight from situations of fear and abuse and 'escape' to the perceived attractions (jobs or "bright lights") elsewhere. However, little is known about the degree to which children who run away from home are at risk of offending. Research by NACRO (1977) found that homeless young offenders are twice as likely to reoffend as those living at home and a recent survey conducted by the Central London Teenage Project found that 11 per cent of the 532 14- to 16- year olds referred to them over a two-year period had been convicted of an offence since leaving home (The Children's Society, 1987).

Parental supervision

In common with an earlier Home Office study of the relationship between parental supervision and delinquency (Riley and Shaw, 1985), this study used a definition of indirect supervision based on parent's knowledge about their children's activities when they are out with their friends. Supervision was measured in terms of what respondents said about whether their parents knew who they were with, and where they were going. Respondents' level of parental supervision was also assessed using the same method as Riley and Shaw (1985). Those respondents who answered "always" to *both* questions were regarded as subject to high supervision and the remainder of the sample were defined as subject to "low/medium" supervision.

Girls were more closely supervised than boys at the age of 14 to 15; 56 per cent were subject to "high" supervision compared with only 28 per cent of boys. For both males and females, supervision was strongly related to offending. Thus, 32 per cent of males and 14 per cent of females who were closely supervised admitted offending compared with 53 per cent and 30 per cent, respectively, of those who were not. These findings are similar to the findings of other research on parental supervision (Wilson, 1980; Riley and Shaw, 1985).

---

3   It is of course not possible to determine causal ordering with cross-sectional data. Getting on badly with a parent or parents may be both a cause and a consequence of youthful misbehaviour. The cyclical and potentially reinforcing nature of poor relationships between parents and their children are in fact difficult to unravel using survey data of any kind, including longitudinal data.

Parental and sibling involvement with the police

Six out of ten respondents knew someone who had been in trouble with the police because they had committed a criminal offence, five out of ten females and seven out of ten males. Knowing people in trouble, whether a parent, friend or acquaintance, was very strongly related to whether the respondent themselves said that they had offended. Within the half of the female population who knew no one in trouble with the police, seven per cent had committed one or more offences at some time in their lives, while among the half who knew people in trouble, 34 per cent had offended. For males the picture is less marked, but still significant – 21 per cent of those who had no contact with people in trouble had ever offended compared with 59 per cent of those who had.

The self report questionnaire was not an ideal method for measuring the involvement of *parents* with the police or, by extension, in crime. Most people who get into trouble with the police do so during their teens and in many cases children will not know whether their parents have ever been in trouble. Consequently, very few respondents reported that their parents had ever been in trouble with the police (2.2 per cent n=29). Although this information is unlikely to be a reliable indicator of parental criminality,[4] it is probably worth noting that among females, the odds of offending of those who thought their parents had been in trouble with the police were nearly four times higher than those who did not ($p<0.01$). For males, parental criminality had no effect on their involvement in offending, but as stated above, this finding cannot be considered reliable. Other research has shown that parental criminality is a strong predictor of delinquency (see, for example, West, 1982) and is closely associated with poor supervision, family discord, unemployment and a host of other family circumstances, all of which are also strong influences on delinquency (Rutter and Giller, 1983).

Respondents were more aware of the involvement of their siblings with the police; about 10 per cent were aware of their brother's or their sister's involvement in crime. Nearly half of the females and nearly three-quarters of the males who had siblings in trouble with the police were offenders themselves. West (1982) reports similar findings for male offenders with brothers in trouble with the police.

School factors

Research has clearly demonstrated that schools play an important role in socialising young people and that academic performance, attendance and behaviour at school are all associated with delinquency (Graham, 1988). The

---

4   It was not possible to obtain data on parental criminality by interviewing parents or checking criminal records for reasons of resource constraints and confidentiality respectively (see introduction).

survey questioned young people on a range of school-related factors, including whether they liked or disliked school, how good they thought they were
at school relative to their peers, whether they truanted from school and
whether they had ever been temporarily or permanently excluded from
school.

Table 4.2
School factors and offending

School factor	males offended		females offended	
	%	(n)	%	(n)
Attachment to school	n.s		****	
high attachment	48	(272)	14	(337)
low attachment	47	(317)	27	(388)
Standard of school work †	n.s.		*	
above average	47	(216)	16	(288)
average/below average	47	(371)	22	(437)
Truanted from school	****		****	
truant	67	(253)	36	(295)
not truant	38	(375)	15	(482)
Temporarily excl. from school	****		***	
excluded	75	(87)	48	(64)
not excluded	45	(542)	20	(716)
Permanently excl. from school	***		**	
excluded	98	(17)	61	(20)
not excluded	47	(611)	20	(763)

weighted percentages, unweighted ns.
n.s.=non-significant *p<0.05 **p<0.01 ***p<0.001 ****p<0.0001
† self-assessed

Attachment to school

Far more respondents liked school than disliked it. To assess the effect of
attachment to school, those who liked school a lot (coded as having high
attachment) were compared with all those who either liked it only a little,
or did not like it at all (coded as having low attachment). Of those females

who liked school, 14 per cent were offenders, whereas of those who liked it a little or not at all, 27 per cent were offenders (p<0.0001). For male offenders, approximately equal proportions (nearly half) liked school a lot as liked school a little or not at all.

Standard of school work

Respondents were asked to assess whether, in their opinion, their school-work was above or below average compared with others in their year at age 14 or 15.[5] About seven per cent of the both males and females rated their school-work to have been "well above average", about one-third rated it above average, 40 per cent said average and about 20 per cent rated themselves as "below" or "well below" average.

Females who rated themselves average or below average were more likely to have offended than those who rated themselves above average (p<0.05). For males, however, no relationship between offending and their assessment of their performance at school (relative to their peers) was found, even among those who rated their performance well below average. This contrasts some-what with the findings from Riley and Shaw (1985) and other similar research (see, for example, Robins, 1966). However, as mentioned above, asking young people to assess their own performance may not be an accu-rate reflection of their actual performance in school and if all those boys who rated themselves as poor were in good schools, any criminogenic effects may be thereby mitigated. These findings should therefore be treated with caution.

Attendance

Non attendance at school or truancy was common among both males and females. Thirty-seven per cent of males and 28 per cent of females said that they had skipped school for at least one day without permission. For both males and females, the odds of offending of those who truanted were more than three times those who had not truanted (p<0.0001) (see Appendix D, Table D1). Those who persistently truanted from school were even more likely to admit offending; 78 per cent of males and 53 per cent of females who truanted once a week or more committed offences. This is in line with other research, which has shown that persistent truants are particularly likely to offend (see, for example, MVA Consultancy, 1991).

---

5   Using school records or interviewing teachers would have provided a more accurate indication of school achieve-ment, but due to resource constraints this was not feasible.

What is less clear is whether truancy leads to delinquency or viceversa. The survey indicated that offending and truancy begin at around the same time in the lives of young people. The average age at which males first truanted from school was 14, while their offending started on average at 13.5, while for females both started at age 13.5 (see Chapter 3, Table 3.4). This does not, however, amount to evidence to support or refute the notion that truancy and delinquency are inter-related.

Exclusions

A minority of both males (11 per cent) and females (4 per cent) had been temporarily excluded from school at some time. Although most were excluded for only a few days, there was a strong relationship between temporary exclusion and offending. Of those males temporarily excluded from school, three-quarters were offenders, whereas of those females temporarily excluded from school, nearly half were offenders.

Permanent exclusion from school was rare, although the effect was far more marked than for temporary exclusions. five out of the eight females who had been permanently excluded from school admitted offending and all of the 11 permanently excluded males admitted offending. The small number of exclusions means, of course, that these findings are tentative, but other research has also found a strong relationship between permanent exclusions and offending (see Graham, 1988).

Clearly, there is a reciprocal relationship between delinquency and exclusion from school. Exclusion is the most serious sanction available to head-teachers and is used in response to problematic behaviour, including theft or violence on school premises, or persistent non-attendance. Since exclusion may be a response to offending, or to behaviour (such as truancy) which is itself related to offending, it is not possible to determine which causes which. It may be more sensible to consider exclusion from school to be both a cause and a consequence of offending. Nevertheless, the chances of committing offences would appear to rise considerably if excluded from school, especially if permanently, and the findings here should be of some concern given the large and increasing numbers of pupils being excluded from school (Lovey *et al*, 1993).

Delinquent peers

As young children become older, peers begin to replace parents as a focus of social approval and status, emotional support and identity formation.

Attachment to peer groups rises in importance as attachment to the family wanes. Research on delinquent peer groups has shown that they are strong influences on whether some young people start offending. Junger-Tas (1988) found very strong associations between self-report offending and having delinquent friends as did West (1982), who reported that more than twice as many offenders were involved in anti-social groups compared with non-offenders. As Table 4.3 illustrates, in this study, nearly three quarters of male offenders and nearly half of female offenders had friends who were in trouble with the police. Only a third of male offenders and less than a sixth of female offenders did not have friends in trouble with the police.

Table 4.3
Friends in trouble with the police and offending (bivariate)

	male offenders		female offenders	
	%	(n)	%	(n)
Friends in trouble with the police ****			****	
in trouble	70	(245)	45	(100)
not in trouble	35	(402)	16	(552)

weighted percentages, unweighted ns.
****p<0.0001

Modelling the onset of offending

So far, through bivariate analyses, a number of factors have been identified as related to the onset of offending. These include relationships with parents and family attachment, parental supervision, parental and sibling criminality, truancy, exclusion from school and association with delinquent peers. Most of these influences applied to both sexes, but there were some factors which were important for girls only, such as social class, liking school and academic performance.

To assess the relative strength of these influences, a multi-variate statistical technique was adopted, logistic regression, which show the results of these analyses for males and females, respectively (see Tables 4.4 and 4.5 over the page).

The variables which remained in the models were similar for both sexes, confirming that the correlates of initial offending are broadly similar for males and females. These results indicate that the three strongest correlates of onset for *both* sexes are contact with delinquent peers, truancy from school and low parental supervision; for both males and females the effect of the variable is strong (that is, substantially increases the probability of offending) and is highly statistically significant. The odds of becoming an offender were nearly four times higher among males who associated with delinquent peers compared with those who did not and nearly six times higher among females who had delinquent peers. Similarly, the odds of becoming an offender were about twice as great among those who were subject to low or medium parental supervision compared with their more highly supervised contemporaries, and the odds of starting to offend of those who had truanted from school were more than twice those who had never truanted.

Table 4.4
Onset of offending: final model (males)

Variable	β		odds ratio	R
Close parental supervision	-0.68	**	-2.0	-0.10
Siblings in trouble with the police	1.09	**	3.0	0.09
Friends in trouble with the police	1.30	****	3.7	0.22
Truanted from school	0.90	****	2.5	0.15
Excluded from school	0.62	†	1.9	0.04

†p<0.1 *p<0.05 **p<0.01 ***p<0.001 ****p<0.0001
Core sample. Unweighted data
499 cases included in final model

Table 4.5
Onset of offending: final model (females)

Variable	β		odds ratio	R
Strongly attached to family	-0.62	*	-1.9	-0.07
Close parental supervision	-0.85	***	-2.3	-0.13
Friends in trouble with the police	1.72	****	5.6	0.25
Truanted from school	0.82	***	2.3	0.13
Strong attachment to school	-0.41	†	-1.5	-0.04

†p<0.1 *p<0.05 **p<0.01 ***p<0.001 ****p<0.0001
Core sample. Unweighted data
603 cases included in final model

For males, two other important correlates of offending were siblings in trouble with the police (three-fold increase in the odds of offending) and exclusions from school (two-fold increase in the odds of offending). For females, low attachment to school (1.5-fold increase in the odds of offending) and low attachment to family (nearly two-fold increase in the odds of offending) were the two remaining correlates of offending in the model. For both males and females, the effect of social class, family structure and family size were not found to be associated with offending once the effects of parental supervision and delinquent peers were taken into account. Likewise, academic performance as rated by respondents in relation to their peers at age 14 and 15, was no longer associated with offending after controlling for truancy and exclusions from school.

Clearly, however, two of the strongest correlates of offending – truancy and association with delinquent peers – are very similar forms of behaviour to offending and need themselves to be explained. To explore this, further multi-variate analysis was conducted, replacing offending as the outcome variable with, firstly, truancy and then secondly with association with delinquent peers.

The correlates of truancy

The correlates of truancy, like offending, were found to be broadly similar for males and females (see Tables D2 and D3, Appendix D). For both sexes, parental supervision, attachment to family and siblings and friends in trouble with the police were all strong correlates of truancy; the first two – weak parental supervision and low family attachment – increased the odds of truanting by between two and three times (since exclusion from school is likely to be closely related to truancy, it was omitted from the modelling). For males, those living in single parent families were also found to be more at risk of truanting, whilst for females those who were not attached to school were more likely to truant. Furthermore, truancy is more common amongst those from social classes III M, IV and V.

Since having delinquent peers is closely related to truancy (i.e. delinquent peers may truant together), the most plausible explanation for truancy would seem to rest on the importance of family influences.[6] Like offenders, truants more often have parents who sometimes do not know where their child is or who they are with, and with whom they have poor relationships.

---

6   Clearly, the quality of the school environment also plays a crucial part in explaining truancy (see Graham, 1988); however, no information was collected on this in the present study.

The correlates of associating with delinquent peers

As might be expected, the strongest correlate of having delinquent peers is truancy. Since truants and those who congregate in delinquent peer-groups may, to a large extent, be the same people, the data was explored for other possible influences on the respondent's association with delinquent peers. This left parental supervision and family structure as the two strongest predictors of association with delinquent peers for both males and females, followed by attachment to family (males only) and attachment to school (females only) (see Tables D4 and D5, Appendix D).

This analysis suggests firstly that parental supervision has a strong *independent* relationship with offending, as well as a strong *indirect* relationship with offending through its close association with truancy and peer delinquency. Parental supervision would seem to be pivotal in promoting or discouraging offending behaviour. Secondly, it suggests that whilst a range of other factors are related to offending (either directly or through their effects on truancy and association with delinquent peers), family attachment also seems to play an important role.

Given the considerable structural changes which families have undergone in the last couple of decades and in particular the increase in single-parent and step-families (see Kiernan and Wicks, 1990), further analysis of the influence of family structure was undertaken. Although family structure was not found to be independently related to offending, its effects may be mediated by truancy, parental supervision and family attachment.

For both males and females, family attachment does indeed vary according to family type. Those who grew up in single-parent families and in step-families were significantly more likely to report having poor relationships with at least one of their parents (including a parent with whom they may not have been living), compared with those brought up by two natural parents. Once family structure is controlled for, social class and family size are not significantly related to family attachment and since parental supervision was found to be only weakly associated with family structure, it appears that it is the existence of a poor relationship between a child and at least one of their parent(s) which explains the higher offending rates in single and step parent families (see Table 4.1). Since the effects of family attachment on offending are mediated by truancy and association with delinquent peers, it can be concluded that young people living in single parent and step-families are more likely to offend because they are more likely to experience problems in their relationships with their parents, which in turn influences their likelihood of truanting from school and associating with delinquent peers.

In sum, therefore, it would appear that the quality of family relationships and the closeness of parental supervision constitute important explanations for a range of problems that arise during adolescence, including truancy from school, contact with delinquent peers and offending itself. Once these factors are taken account of, social class and family size have no significant relationship with offending, whilst family structure remains indirectly related to offending through its influence on the capacity of parents to build and maintain good relationships with their children and to carefully supervise where and with whom they spend their time outside the home.

Adverse factors and delinquency

Another way to express the relative importance of family, school and other variables is to consider each of the most important correlates as an 'adverse factor'. Counting each of five most important family and school attributes – delinquent peers, low parental supervision, truancy from school, and (for males) delinquent siblings and exclusion from school or (for females) weak attachment to family and school – as an adverse factor provides a possible score ranging from nought to five.

Table 4.6
Adverse factors and offending (males)

Number of adverse factors	N	Proportion delinquent
		%
0	125	20
1	188	36
2	162	62
3	107	71
4 or 5	50	81

core sample, weighted data

Table 4.6 shows that as the adverse factor score increases, so does the proportion of males who admitted ever committing a criminal offence. Thus, while one in five of those who had no adverse factors admitted offending, among those with the highest scores more than eight out of ten were delinquent. Equivalent results for females are presented in Table 4.7. This analysis shows that less than one in ten females with no adverse factors admitted offending, whilst more than six out of ten of those with the highest scores admitted offending.

Table 4.7
Adverse factors and offending (females)

Number of adverse factors	N	Proportion delinquent
		%
0	163	7
1	218	13
2	189	27
3	142	35
4 or 5	89	61

core sample, weighted data

Sex differences in offending

The variables included in the model of onset of offending each vary by sex. Considering family and school factors for example, girls were much more closely supervised than boys, they were significantly less likely to have truanted from school, to have been excluded or to have associated with delinquent peers. Given these gender differences, it might be that these factors explain the difference between the rate of participation in offending between girls and boys. To test this possibility, sex was introduced into the final model of onset to see the extent to which a sex difference would remain after controlling for the influences of family, school and other relevant factors. The results indicated that after controlling for these influences, sex itself remained an important variable. Among those males and females who are equally closely supervised at home and at school, who are equally attached to their school and their family and who have no delinquent peers, offending remains about twice as common among males as females. This suggests that there must be other influences on male offenders – be they biological, psychological or sociological – which are not included in this study. Future research may help to discover what these influences might be.

Summary and conclusions

The results presented in this chapter confirm other research evidence which indicates that the family and the school each play an important part in explaining why boys and girls start to commit criminal offences. There appears to be only a weak relationship between starting to offend and both the social class and the structure of the family in which the respondent was brought up; it is the effect of relationships within the family that appears to have the greatest bearing on whether an individual commits a criminal offence. The teenagers and young adults interviewed who didn't get on with one or other of their parents, were subject to low parental supervision (thought their parents sometimes didn't know where they were or who they were with) or had run away from home, were much more likely to have committed a criminal offence. Once these characteristics of the relationship between parents and children had been controlled for, the relatively small effects of social class, family size and family structure disappeared.

A strong association between non-attachment to school and offending was also found. The odds of offending of those who truanted from school were three times higher than those who did not truant. Similarly, there is a very strong correlation between exclusions and offending. Offending was more common among girls who didn't like school or who thought that their school work was average or below for their year, though these factors had no effect on boys.

Taking both family and school factors together, parental supervision and truancy from school emerged as the two strongest correlates of starting to offend. Furthermore, parental supervision was also found to be a strong predictor of truancy. Thus those teenagers who spend considerable periods of time unsupervised by either their parents or the school are more likely to engage in truancy and criminal activity than those who are not. However, a low level of parental supervision was found to be strongly related to getting on badly with one or both parents, which in turn was found to be more likely in single parent and step families. The higher offending rates of children in single parent and step families are therefore explained by the higher likelihood of them experiencing a poor relationship with one or both of their parents.

In addition to the relationships between family, school and offending, a very strong correlate of offending was having friends who were in trouble with the police (used as an indication of peer delinquency). The odds of offending was three times greater among those with delinquent peers, even after controlling for the effects of other influences. Although this confirms the findings of earlier research (e.g. Riley and Shaw, 1985), concerns about the order of any causal relationship between delinquent peers and offending must be borne in mind. Rather than associating with delinquents causing an individual to offend, it might be that delinquents merely flock together, perhaps supporting delinquency but not necessarily giving rise to it in the first place.

5 The transition to adulthood and desistance from offending

The last chapter identified some of the main explanations for why some young people start offending. This chapter examines the notion that most young offenders tend to grow out of crime and identifies the main factors associated with desistance from offending. The chapter is divided into three sections. In the first section evidence is presented on the relationship between desistance from offending and personal and social development within the context of the transition from childhood to adulthood. The second part examines this relationship for specific age groups and for different types of offence. The third section offers alternative explanations for why some young people desist from offending during the period of transition to adulthood, whilst others do not.

As part of the survey, every respondent who said that they had committed an offence "ever" was asked whether they thought they would do so again in the future and if so, why. Of those who admitted to committing at least one offence in the past, approximately two-thirds said they would not do so again in the future. Their responses are presented in Table 5.1 below.

Table 5.1
Reasons given for not committing an offence again

Reason	Males	Females
	%	%
It's childish	24	26
The risk of getting caught	21	18
It's wrong	15	14
My life has changed	10	8
It's pointless	7	8
What people would think of me	4	2
I have different friends now	2	4
Someone might do the same to me	4	1
I have enough money now	2	2
I have a child	1	3
Other	7	11
Don't know	3	3
Unweighted N	234	214

core sample, weighted percentages.

In general, the picture looks similar for males and females. Looking at the most common responses, roughly one-quarter of both males and females said that they wouldn't offend again because they thought what they had done was "childish" and roughly one-fifth of each mentioned the "risk of getting caught"; one-seventh said that they wouldn't do it again simply because it was wrong and one-tenth because their life had changed. There were some sex differences among the less common reasons given for desisting. Young women were more likely to mention the fact that they had children and much less likely to have stopped because they feared that they would suffer retaliation. These findings only represent what respondents thought they would do in the future. However, beliefs do not necessarily coincide with what happens in reality, so a more sophisticated and objective attempt was made to assess the reasons why some young people might desist from, as opposed to persist with, offending.

Defining "desisters"

In order to analyse desistance from offending it was first necessary to exclude those defined in Chapter 4 as "non-offenders" and minor "one-off offenders". The remaining respondents, who were identified as "ever offenders", were defined as "desisters" if they had committed at least three offences (or one serious offence) in the past, but had not committed an offence for at least 12 months prior to the interview. A total of 166 desisters were thus identified, along with 226 persisters (those who had not only committed at least three offences [or one serious offence] in the past, but had also committed at least one offence in the last 12 months).

Admitting to not offending for a period of at least one year is clearly a better indicator of desistance than not being officially *recorded* as having committed an offence for at least a year, since recorded desisters may have offended without having been caught. But to ensure that the one year period was sufficient, analysis was also conducted on a sample of desisters who had refrained from offending for longer (two and three years). The results were broadly similar. Another definition of desistance, which required a period of desistance longer than the interval between offences, was tried and this also produced similar results. Since the number of desisters using a one-year period produced a larger sample (which increases the chances of establishing whether the findings are due to chance or not), this definition was chosen for the final analysis. In practice of course, most desisters (particularly older respondents) had desisted for considerably longer than one year – the average period of desistance was four years.[1] Given that this is self-report rather than conviction data (and

---

1   The average period of desistance for 14- to 17-year-olds was approximately 2.5 years, for 18- to 21-year-olds 3.5 years and for 22- to 25-year-olds 6 years (weighted data).

thus avoids possible measurement error associated with the detection of offences), it seems reasonable to argue that most of those identified as desisters will actually have stopped offending.

Analysing desistance

To test the hypothesis that desistance from offending is related to personal and social development or "growing out of crime", the survey included a number of questions relating to the main transitional life events experienced by young people as they proceed from childhood to adulthood. The personal and social development factors explored were completing full-time education, taking up stable employment, leaving home, getting married/forming stable relationship, staying in to look after children and taking responsibility for themselves and for others. In the interests of clarity, these factors are referred to as social development factors henceforth.

In order to explore the influence of these factors on desistance from offending, the study looked firstly at how young men and women make this transition and in particular at what age these transitional landmarks are passed (if at all). Having compared the timing of each transition for both males and females, relationships are then explored between changes in patterns of offending and changes in the developmental situation of young people as they grow into adults. In order to allow for the fact that some of these transitions are more likely or only likely to occur at specific ages (e.g. acquiring stable employment and marriage will not affect the youngest respondents), all analyses were also conducted on each of three four-year age groups. The results were the same as for the whole age range in virtually every case, but with one or two notable differences (see below).

The next step, as with the analysis of onset in the last chapter, comprised an analysis of the bivariate associations between stopping offending and the indicators of social development mentioned above. To simplify the analysis and presentation of this information, each social development variable was dichotomised. As a consequence, some information was lost. For example, by comparing those who were in work against those who were not, people in full-time education, youth training, economically inactive etc. needed to be lumped together into the "not in full-time employment" category. The associations between desistance and each dichotomised social development variable are presented below in Table 5.2. Finally, models incorporating the strongest variables were constructed in order to explore the relative importance of the different factors (see Tables D4.6 and D4.7, Appendix D).

Social development and the transition from childhood to adulthood

The above list of social development variables were explored in terms of when, on average, each transition is made and what proportions of males and females achieved each transition by specific ages.

Completing full time education and taking up stable employment

While only about one in five 16- to 17-year-olds had left full-time education, more than half had done so by the age of 18 to 19 and by age 24 to 25, 80 per cent of males and 97 per cent of females had completed full-time education. Taking up stable full-time employment[2] lags some way behind leaving school. One in ten 16- to 17-year-olds are in full-time employment as were about one quarter of female and one-third of male 18- to 19-year-olds. Among the 20 to 23 year olds sampled more females than males were in full-time employment, though this position changed by age 24 to 25 when just over half of the males and one-third of females were in stable full-time employment.

Leaving home and attaining economic independence

Nearly all 14- to 19-year-olds were living at home at the time of the survey, but by the age of 20 to 21, about 30 per cent of males and 40 per cent of females had left home. By age 24 to 25, nearly two-thirds of males and three-quarters of females had left home. Those respondents who said that they themselves usually paid for their own food, clothing, travel and entertainment were defined as being economically independent. Approximately four per cent of 16- to 17-year-olds were economically independent, as were about one fifth of 18- to 19-year-olds. In the 20 to 21 age group, 40 per cent of females and one third of males were economically independent, whilst in the 22 to 23 age group nearly half of the females (but only 30 per cent of the males) were so. By the age of 24 to 25, just over half of all the young people in the study were still not economically independent.

Forming stable partnerships/getting married

Compared with males, females were much more likely to have formed a stable pair-relationship or be married by their twenties, and among those who were single, females were much more likely to have had a relationship

---

2   Those who said that they were in full-time employment (over 30 hours per week) were also asked whether they enjoyed the job and what they thought they would be doing in 12 months' time. All those in employment who liked (or at least tolerated) their job and expected to still be employed by the end of the year were coded as being in stable full-time work.

in the past. While only two per cent of the males in the sample were living with a partner by age 18 to 19, eight per cent of the females were. By age 24 to 25 just over half of the females were living as married compared with barely a quarter of the males. A similar picture is true for marriage *per se* with 42 per cent of the women, but only 16 per cent of the men married by age 24 to 25.

Responsibility for oneself, for children and for others

A measure of responsibility for self was constructed using information about the extent to which respondents always, usually or (at least) sometimes took responsibility for household food shopping, washing up, cleaning their own room, making beds, meals or washing clothes. Again there was a marked sex difference, especially among older respondents, with more than twice as many females aged 24 to 25 meeting their own domestic responsibilities as males.

Perhaps the greatest responsibility that may be faced during this transitional phase is having children of one's own. Again, males lag some way behind females. No males in the sample had children before the age of 18 compared with three per cent of females and while seven per cent of young women aged 18 to 19 had children, only one per cent of males did. These figures rise gradually with males consistently lagging behind by two or three years until, by the age of 24 to 25, approximately half of the women had children compared with one-quarter of the men.[3]

In order that our indicator of parental responsibility did not include those who had children but took little or no responsibility for them, those who stayed in most evenings to look after them were defined as having responsibility for children. As might be expected, females were much more likely than males to spend most evenings at home looking after their children. Among 24- to 25-year-olds, 42 per cent of women stayed in to look after their children compared with 10 per cent of men.

Finally, a measure of responsibility for others was constructed using information on whether the respondent helped other people by, for example, cooking, cleaning, looking after elderly relatives, or doing painting, decorating or repairs around the house. Males were not only less likely to take on such responsibilities than females, but when they did, they lagged behind them in doing so. By the mid-20s, about one-third of males were taking on such responsibilities, whereas more than half of the females were doing so at this age.

---

3   Data from the 1991 census shows that about 37 per cent of females aged 25 or under have one or more children, which suggests that the sample of females in this study is biased towards those with children (OPCS, 1994).

Social development and desistance from offending

The above shows that many young people, even by their mid-twenties, have still not completed the transition to a fully independent adult life. The findings of other research suggests that the period of adolescence has lengthened and changed markedly over the last 50 years (for an overview, see Leffert and Petersen, 1995). The findings of this study suggest that this applies in particular to young men, who tend to lag behind young women in virtually every area of social development. If it is true that young people grow out of crime, then many will fail to do so, at least by their mid-twenties, simply because they have not been able to grow up, let alone grow out of crime. To test this premise, an analysis of the relationship between these social development variables and desistance from offending was undertaken (see Table 5.2).

Table 5.2
Social development and desistance from offending

Indicator of social development	Males				Females			
	% desisted	odds†	s.s.	(n)	% desisted	odds†	s.s.	(n)
Completed education	32	-1.6	n.s.	(132)	54	3.9	*	(103)
In stable full-time employment	25	-2.2	n.s.	(60)	54	2.2	n.s.	(18)
Lives at home	41	1.6	n.s.	(175)	29	-1.8	**	(99)
Economically independent	38	1.0	n.s.	(51)	76	7.0	*	(29)
Married	64	3.1	n.s.	(10)	100	§	***	(12)
Lives with a partner	32	-1.3	n.s.	(24)	90	20.1	****	(22)
Stays in to look after children	18	-2.8	n.s.	(11)	63	3.4	*	(35)
Takes responsibility for self	62	2.9	n.s.	(12)	51	1.8	n.s.	(36)
Takes responsibility for others	45	1.4	n.s.	(47)	52	2.1	n.s.	(57)
Mean	38			(236)	38			(156)

Weighted percentages, unweighted ns., significance tests on unweighted data

n.s.=non-significant; *p<.05; **p<.0.01; ***p<0.001; ****p<0.0001

† The odds value or ratio provides an indication of the increase or decrease in the odds of offending for respondents for whom the item shown in the column marked "indicator of social development" applies. A positive odds value indicates an increased probability of desistance and a negative odds value a decreased probability.

§ An odds ratio cannot be computed when the percentage desisted=100.

Completing full-time education and taking up stable employment

Among females, the odds of desisting from offending were nearly four times more for those who had left education compared with those still in full-time education. For males, however, desistance was no more likely among those still in education compared with those who had left. The effect of taking up stable full-time employment had no effect on the likelihood of either males or females desisting from offending, although the number of females in full-time employment is small.[4]

Leaving home and attaining economic independence

The effects of leaving home had opposite effects for males and females. The odds that females who had left home would desist from offending were nearly twice those still living with their parents, whereas leaving home had no significant effect on the likelihood of desisting among males. The effect of economic independence was also quite different for males and females. The odds of those females who were economically independent desisting from offending were about seven times greater than for those who were economically dependent. For males, however, economic independence made no significant difference to their likelihood of desisting.

Forming stable partnerships/getting married

Those females who were married were the most likely to have desisted from offending (100 per cent), followed by those living as married (90 per cent). Those in relationships longer than one year (but not cohabiting) were less likely than average to have desisted (33 per cent) and those in relationships of less than one year fell between the two (55 per cent). For males, those who had never had a relationship with a girl were most likely to desist (53 per cent), followed by those who were married or living as married (46 per cent). Those in relationships longer than one year who were not living together were the most likely to have persisted with offending (28 per cent). The effect of relationships for males, however, was not statistically significant.

---

4   Since the employment variable is dichotomised, those not in stable full-time employment do not simply comprise the unemployed. Those *not* in stable full-time employment include those in education, training and part time employment, as well as the unemployed. Thus the logistic regression analysis does not show whether young offenders are less (or indeed more) likely to desist from offending as a consequence of being unemployed. It is possible that the effect of unemployment on desistance is cancelled out by the effect of the increase in opportunities for committing offences when in work (i.e. theft from the workplace and fraud). It is also possible that the effect of obtaining stable employment on desistance will vary according to the aggregate level of employment amongst young people at any one moment in time (see Smith, 1995).

Responsibility for oneself, for children and for others

Neither self-reliance, nor taking responsibility for others were related to desistance from offending for either sex. However, the odds of those females who took responsibility for children stopping offending were around three times higher than for those who did not (p<0.05), whereas responsibility for looking after children had no significant effect on males.

Taken separately, it is apparent that most of the indicators of social development are strongly related to desistance for females, but not for males. For females, each indicator of social development is statistically significant at the five per cent level or higher, except for taking up stable full-time employment and taking responsibility for self and others. The change in the relative chance of desistance on passing each developmental "landmark" indicates that each of the statistically significant effects is also quite marked. The strongest effects are that of marriage and forming partnerships. All of those women who were married had stopped offending while among those who were living as married, the odds of desisting were more than twenty times the odds of desisting among those who were single (p<0.0001).

For males, none of the indicators of social development were found to be statistically significant. The variable most likely to exert an effect on desistance among males was marriage, which increases the odds of desistance for males by a factor of three. However, because so few males in the sample were married (4.2 per cent), this finding fell some way short of statistical significance (p= 0.17).

Desistance among different age groups

The data presented so far considers desistance among all respondents taken together, irrespective of their age. However, by aggregating all ages into one age span, the effects of specific social development factors within a smaller age range may be cancelled out. For example, having children at the age of 17 or 18 may have very different effects on the likelihood of desisting than having children at the age of 24 or 25. Similarly, young offenders may be influenced towards desisting by obtaining stable employment during their mid-twenties, but not during their mid-teens. Indeed, given that social development factors do not seem to explain desistance for males over the whole of this age span, it is important to see whether they may have some influence during any part of it. As males appear to reach adulthood later than females, it may be that the effects of social development factors begin to be discernible among the 22 to 25 year age group. To test the possible interaction effects of age, the relationship between desistance and these developmental landmarks were examined within three age groups: 14 to 17s, 18 to

21s and 22 to 25s. (Because of small numbers, some of the factors which are significant for the overall age range are no longer significant even though the magnitude of the effect is the same or larger; only significant findings are presented.)

For females, the effects of social development are broadly consistent among each age group, though some variables had a different effect at different ages. Thus, for 14- to 17-year-olds leaving school was the only statistically significant finding, whilst living with a partner and marriage are strong predictors of desistance for those in their twenties. Although the correlates of desistance do vary to some extent depending on the age of the respondent, the overall effect of social development between the age of 14 and 25 remains clear for females. The overall correspondence between patterns of offending and the transition to adulthood in terms of timing and strong statistically significant association suggests that the two processes are closely interrelated.

The data for males, when broken down by age category, also tends to confirm the picture for the whole age range. The only statistically significant finding was that older males who still lived at home were found to be nearly twice as likely to desist than those who had left home. Thus for males, desisters and persisters were simply too similar in terms of their social development for any conclusions to be drawn, even once they reached their mid-twenties. It seems plausible, therefore, to suggest that if young men do desist from offending as a consequence of "growing" out of crime, many are likely to do so only *after* the age of 25.

Desistance from different types of offence

The analysis so far has been based on overall offending. However, as described in Chapters 2 and 3, property and violent offences have somewhat different distributions by age, sex, etc. It is therefore possible that the correlates of desistance may be different for different types of offences, although the overlap between offence types is considerable – those who committed one type of offence were also likely to commit other types of offence. The same was found for stopping offending. That is, those who had desisted from one type of offence were also likely to have stopped committing other types of offence.

Nevertheless, in order to check whether the correlates of desistance were the same or different for violent offences, acquisitive property offences, and damage to property (graffiti, vandalism and arson), desistance from each was analysed separately. The results of this analysis indicated that, broadly speaking, the correlates of desistance were similar for each. As the analysis of desistance from all offending indicated, for each different type of offending, social development variables were strong correlates of desistance for females but not for males.

Modelling desistance from offending

The above analysis of desistance has shown that, on the basis of bivariate analyses differentiating by age groups and offence types, the likelihood that females will desist from crime increases if they have made various life transitions, but that these transitions are of little significance for males, at least up to the age of 25. To assess the relative strength of the social development variables for males and females separately a logistic regression analysis was carried out using the same method as in Chapter 4 (see Appendix D).

The resulting regression model for females (see Table D7, Appendix D), reflects the findings from the bivariate analysis, confirming that completing full-time education, becoming economically independent and forming a partnership are strong and statistically significant correlates of desistance from offending. As girls grow into young women so their likelihood of desisting from crime increases. Given the obvious inter-relationship between age and social development, the effect of age *per se* was tested by re-introducing age into the model in a number of ways (see Appendix E). This analysis indicated that the effect of chronological age was not significantly related to desistance after taking account of the effect of developmental influences.

The same analysis was conducted for males and produced very different results (Table D6, Appendix D). The overall performance of the model was poor and the only significant developmental variable in the model was leaving home, and this *reduced* rather than increased the likelihood of desisting from offending. It would appear, then, that those young men who continue to be subject to the control and supervision of their parents are more likely to desist from offending than those who do not. Those who are released, or who release themselves, into a world in which these constraining influences no longer prevail are at a greater risk of continuing to offend.

The only other variable which was significant in the model of desistance among males was chronological age. As males grow older, so the likelihood of most desisting from offending increases. However, since chronological age has little if any meaning in and of itself (see Rutter, 1989 and Appendix E, which comprises a more detailed if rather technical discourse on the relationship between age and offending), there must be other factors which influence young men who offend to desist or persist as they grow older.

Whilst young men may not, at the aggregate level, pass into adulthood as quickly or as comprehensively as females, at least some of them will acquire a sense of responsibility and a degree of independence and autonomy by the time they reach their mid-twenties. The question remains, therefore, that if social development variables do little to explain desistance from offending for males, what does? This question was addressed in two ways – by looking at the influence of the correlates of onset and by exploring the survey data for other possible influences on desistance.

The correlates of desistance as the obverse of the correlates of onset

The factors which influence desistance may simply be the *obverse* of the same factors which influence them to offend in the first place. In other words, desistance could be influenced by positive early influences in the home and at school. To test this possibility, a second set of models were constructed containing the family, school and peer-group variables used to investigate the onset of offending – attachment to family, parental supervision, involvement of siblings in crime, truancy, attachment to school, standard of school work and association with delinquent peers.

The resulting model for males indicated that the odds of desisting of those without delinquent peers were around three times higher than those who associated with delinquent peers (p<0.002). Similarly, the odds of desisting from offending for those who had an above average self-assessed standard of school work were three times those who performed averagely or below at school (p<0.003). This model performed adequately but a great deal of variance remained to be explained (see Appendix D, Table D8). When the model of onset was applied to the female sample, none of the variables were found to be significantly associated with desistance. This indicates that for females, the obverse of those factors which are strong influences on starting to offend have no influence on the likelihood of desistance.

Since the obverse of those variables which explain the onset of offending *do not* adequately explain desistance among males, it seemed likely that there must be a number of additional factors coming into play after onset which sustain a deviant lifestyle. The survey data were therefore trawled for other possible influences on desistance which are neither the obverse of onset nor constitute social development variables.

Risk factors, social development and desistance

Using crosstabulation, the strongest bivariate correlates of desistance for males were identified and are shown in Table 5.3. These variables concerned their victimisation, the frequency of their prior offending, whether their siblings, partners or peers had been in trouble with the police, whether they were heavy drinkers, and whether they used hard drugs in the past year.

Table 5.3
Risk factors and desistance from offending (males and females shown separately)

Risk factors	Males				Females			
	% desisted	odds†	s.s.	(n)	% desisted	odds†	s.s.	(n)
Victim of violence (last 12 months)	28	-1.8	*	(72)	22	-2.8	n.s.	(32)
Ever committed 5 offences or fewer	46	1.8	*	(98)	58	7.4	****	(86)
(Ex-)Partner in trouble with police	20	-2.6	*	(23)	41	1.2	n.s.	(57)
Siblings in trouble with police	15	-4.0	*	(38)	43	1.3	n.s.	(38)
Friends in trouble with the police	30	-2.2	***	(140)	39	1.1	n.s.	(65)
Heavy drinker	20	-3.3	*	(41)	18	-2.9	n.s.	(17)
Hard drug use	22	-2.4	**	(52)	48	1.7	n.s.	(30)
Mean	26			(236)	38			(156)

weighted percentages, unweighted ns., significance tests on unweighted data
n.s.=non-significant; *p<0.05; **p<0.01; ***p<0.001; ****p<0.0001
† The odds value or ratio provides an indication of the increase or decrease in the odds of offending for respondents who have experienced or are exposed to the items shown in the column marked "risk factors". A positive odds value indicates an increased probability of desistance and a negative odds value a decreased probability.

These bivariate results indicate that the odds of desisting from crime for male offenders were considerably lower if they had siblings who were in trouble with the police (by a factor of 4), where they had a partner or ex-partner who was in trouble with the police (by a factor of 2.6), where they were heavy drinkers (by a factor of 3.3), where they had used hard drugs in the past year (by a factor of 2.4) and where they had committed five or more offences or been a victim of violence in the previous year (both by a factor of 1.8). All these results were statistically significant for males.

In order to test the relative influence of these variables, a model comprising these correlates of desistance, together with the social development variables, was fitted to the data for males and females separately. The results for males are presented in Table 5.4.

Table 5.4
Final model of desistance (males)

Variable	β	odds ratio	R
Aged 20 or older	0.9**	2.6	0.14
(Ex-)Partner in trouble with police	-1.7*	-5.5	-0.10
Siblings in trouble with the police	-1.0*	-2.8	-0.08
Friends in trouble with the police	-1.0**	-2.8	-0.17
Heavy drinker	-1.0*	-2.8	-0.09
Hard drug user	-0.9*	-2.4	-0.08
Above average at school	0.8*	2.2	0.11

194 cases in final model
*p<.05 **p<.0.01 ***p<0.001 ****p<0.0001
a negative value for the odds ratio indicates a decreased probability of desistance

After including risk factors, the protective effect of school achievement remained robust, but the protective effect of living at home was reduced substantially and only approached statistical significance ($p=0.17$). Of the risk factors, those who had a high rate of prior offending were less likely to desist, those whose partner, ex-partner or siblings had been in trouble with the police were less likely to desist, as were those who took drugs or drank heavily. Nevertheless, age still remained an important explanatory variable.[5] This final model performed well.

Unlike social development variables, these factors do seem to influence desistance from offending among males insofar as they *sustain* involvement in criminal activities. Insofar as young males can resist or avoid these influences, they will avoid their criminogenic effects and foster desistance from offending. For females, only one of these risk factors entered the final model – frequency of prior offending. Together with completing education and forming partnerships, these three factors produced a model which performed better than the model restricted to social development variables

---

5 Victimisation was only measured in terms of violence. This might account for the fact that victimisation falls out of the overall model for desistance. If other forms of victimisation had been included, victimisation may well have been one of the main predictors of persistence, as found by Aye Maung (1995). Further analysis is being conducted on the predictors of violence and desistance from violent offending, which will hopefully confirm or otherwise the predictive effect of victimisation.

due to the powerful influence of prior offending on current offending (see Table D9, Appendix D).

Although the risk factors referred to above reduce the likelihood of desistance from offending among males, they may themselves have antecedent relationships with family and socio-demographic factors. To explore this possibility a model was constructed for each risk factor in turn. The analysis showed that those who associated with other offenders (whether siblings, friends, a partner or an ex-partner) also had poor quality relationships with their parents. Additionally, those who continued to live at home were also found to have good relationships with their parents and not to have siblings in trouble with the police. Thus although the quality of family relationships does not *directly* influence the likelihood of desistance from offending, it does *indirectly* affect desistance by delaying the onset of offending during the teenage years and allowing young people to stay at home, largely without undue inter-personal stresses, which in turn inhibits them to some extent from associating with other offenders.

Discussion and conclusions

The findings presented above indicate that females are less likely than males ever to start to offend and desist sooner than their male counterparts. Females are also more likely than males to acquire the symbols of adult status by the time they reach their early twenties. The data also suggest that the transition to adulthood and desistance from offending are closely associated for females; as girls become women, leave home and school, form partnerships and new families and become economically independent, so they desist from offending. Importantly, once social development is accounted for, chronological age *per se* has little if any explanatory value.

Males, however, are less likely than their female counterparts to achieve the independence, responsibility and maturity associated with adulthood by the age of 25. They tend, even by the age of 24 to 25, to be dependent rather than independent, to have an absence of responsibility for themselves and others and to remain with their family of origin rather than forming a family of their own. The period of transition for males not only starts later, but is longer and, for many, still incomplete by their mid-twenties.

Contrary to initial expectations, social development variables are less (if at all) useful in explaining desistance among males (but see Chapter 6 below). Those males who had left home, formed partnerships and had children were no more likely to have desisted than those who had not made these life transitions. Thus, it appears to be the case that not only do many young men fail to successfully make the transition to adulthood by their mid-twenties, those who do appear to be no more likely to desist than those who do not. Rather, failing to desist (or continuing to persist with offending) may be better explained by three sets of risk factors. Firstly, those who have a high frequency of prior offending are much more likely to persist with offending than their counterparts who only ever offended infrequently (the same would also seem to apply to females, but to a lesser degree). Secondly, those who maintain contact with delinquent peers are much more likely to continue to offend than those who break away from a delinquent peer-group. Thirdly, those who drink heavily and use controlled drugs are more likely to persist than non-drinkers and non-drug users.

Two protective factors also emerge from the study. Firstly, those who had a good relationship with their parents during their adolescence and young adulthood and continued to live at home were more likely to desist than those who had problems at home and left home early. However, this protective factor may be overwhelmed by the effects of the risk factors mentioned above. Secondly, those whose standard of school work was self-assessed to be above average were more likely to desist than their counterparts. This indicates that a successful school career can, later, have the benefit of reducing the likelihood of persisting with offending.

This leaves two questions unanswered. Firstly, why do those males who seem to have made the transition from childhood to adulthood within this 12-year period appear to be no more likely to have desisted from offending than those who have not made this transition?

One possibility, as suggested by Laub and Sampson (1993), is that transitions like marriage and employment might not have the same meaning for every one and only provide *opportunities* for change to occur; its realisation is mediated by individual contingencies. Males may be less inclined to grasp, or be able to take advantage of such opportunities, as females. One reason for this might be that the negative payoff of embracing these opportunities may outweigh the positive outcomes for males, but not for females. An example of this might be having children.

Alternatively, it may be that the effect of passing these developmental landmarks is overwhelmed by other more powerful influences. It certainly seems to be the case that males who continue to have contact with delinquent peers, drink heavily and take hard drugs are more likely to continue to offend than those who do not. It may be that young men, irrespective of whether they are objectively more "mature", are unable to detach themselves from offending behaviour whilst still remaining in contact with friends and family members who are themselves in trouble with the police, drink heavily and use drugs.

That patterns of social development and desistance from offending during the transition to adulthood should be closely linked in the lives of young women, while having no clear link in the lives of young men poses questions concerning the significance of gender roles in the 1990s. The "end-point" that marks the conventional definition of the end of childhood and the certainty of adult status appears to have become more distant for (most obviously) men and (to a lesser extent) women. Certainly for young men, the shift from starting work straight after school to delaying entry into the world of work until well into the twenties is likely to have profoundly affected the daily life routines and outlook of the current young generation.

Whether these changes are impacting upon the offending careers of young people and if so in what way has been the central concern of this chapter. The next chapter explores these issues in more depth through interviews with a small sub-sample of desisters.

6 Explaining desistance from offending

In the previous chapter, a number of factors were identified as associated with desistance from offending. For females, leaving school and forming a new family were found to be strong correlates of desistance. For males, on the other hand, these factors were not found to be associated with desistance. Whether or not young male offenders stop offending would seem to be associated with a number of criminogenic influences characteristic of their lives during this period. However the survey data are unable to fully explain how and why desistance occurs for some offenders and not others and what the social and cognitive *processes* are which lead to desistance. Why is leaving school strongly related to desistance for girls? Why do some boys manage to stop offending in spite of the powerful influences on them to continue? A limited attempt to illuminate these and other questions relating to the detailed experiences of the lives of young desisters are addressed below.

In order to discover more about the actual processes which lead to desistance, a small sub-sample of desisters were identified from the survey and interviewed in-depth. The interviews allowed individual desisters to describe the circumstances which led to involvement in offending and later to desistance in the context of the main personal and social developments in their lives as teenagers and young adults. Through these retrospective life-history accounts, it was possible to track events over time and identify the influences, conditions and circumstances which ultimately led them to desisting from offending.

Methodology

Interviewees were defined as desisters if they had committed three or more relatively serious offences at some point in the past, but had not committed any offences within the past year.[1] A sample drawn from those who had consented to being re-contacted when first interviewed was selected on the basis of their age, their sex and the characteristics of their prior offending. In total, 42 respondents were invited by letter to a second interview and of these 21 were subsequently re-interviewed. Of those with whom second

---

1   Drug offences were omitted from this analysis since the distribution of these offences differs markedly from the other offence groups included (see Chapter 1).

interviews were not achieved, six refused to be interviewed and 15 could not be located. All interviews were fully tape recorded and all statements are taken verbatim from interview transcripts.

Ten males and 11 females aged 16 to 27 were re-interviewed. They had committed a wide range of different types of offences, with varying degrees of frequency and seriousness. The process of desistance will vary according to the type of offence but the interviewees had mostly committed similar offences and did not tend to specialise in any one particular type of crime.

Each respondent was interviewed for between 45 and 90 minutes using a semi-structured interview schedule. The interview focused on what respondents perceived to be the most important developments in their lives, focusing in particular on:

- the transition from school to college, work, training or unemployment

- moving away from home and establishing an independent living space

- losing and gaining friendships

- forming relationships with the opposite sex and having children

- the use of leisure time and the consumption of alcohol and drugs.

The interviews are necessarily subjective accounts which are prone to distortion in a number of ways. Since they are retrospective accounts, their accuracy will be affected by the quality of the respondents' memories of (often long-past) experiences and events. These events may also have been subjected to differing degrees of reconstruction and redefinition. Explanations which follow some time after an event may therefore be partly improvised or speculative. A degree of validity could have been achieved by conducting comparable interviews with non-offenders and non-desisters, but the resources for this were not available.

In contrast to the survey, the in-depth interviews provide detailed information on a small number of individuals rather than a limited amount of information on a large number of people. They can be used to illustrate a much wider range of influences on behaviour, but of course what applies to one individual may not apply to another. The survey highlighted the likely influences on desistance at the aggregate *population* level; the in-depth interviews only explain desistance at the *individual* level and even then only for a small, not necessarily typical, sample. Having said this, the interviews produced some striking similarities in terms of life experiences and whilst each case is different in its detail, a number of common threads can be identified which permeate the lives of young desisters. As will be seen, there are still some individual males for whom social development can impact upon their offending behaviour.

The interviews provided information on how the process of desistance actually unfolds. Some offenders stopped quite suddenly, either by making a conscious decision to do so or due to radical changes, fortuitous or otherwise, in their circumstances. Others desist gradually, intermittently and often unconsciously with changes in their circumstances and behaviour. For them, the process of desistance may be sporadic, with periods of offending interspersed between periods of desistance.

Some of the people identified as desisters – that is said that they had not offended within the year prior to the survey – had reoffended since the first interview, which was conducted eighteen months earlier. It is of course possible that others may offend in the future. So whilst some interviewees could not be defined with any certainty as permanent desisters, they all provided useful explanations for their attempts to give up offending. In some cases there had been a reduction in frequency or seriousness, whilst in others there was a genuine belief that they had to all intents and purposes given up offending, with just the occasional lapse.

The remainder of this chapter describes and explains the process of desistance in the context of the development of responsibility and maturity on the basis of the interviewees' own narrative accounts.

Personal and social development and desistance from offending

On the basis of a careful analysis of the interviews with desisters, four principal mechanisms or processes can be identified as influencing desistance:[2]

(i) Disassociation from offenders

(ii) Forming stable relationships and having children

(iii) Acquiring a sense of direction

(iv) Realising in time or learning the hard way.

---

2   These four processes can (and no doubt do) overlap and should not be considered as distinct alternatives.

Disassociation from delinquent peers

A key thread running through the interviewees' accounts of how they stopped offending, as found in the previous chapter, concerned their disassociation from other offenders. In some cases it was an ex-partner or a sibling, but in most cases it was their peer group. Disengaging from delinquent peers, whether consciously or by chance, is a necessary condition for desistance and may occur in a number of ways. The simplest is when a parent or sibling intervenes to bring about such a change. Much of one interviewee's offending, for example, was committed with one specific friend and only ended when his brother acted to end the relationship.

> *He was a close friend at the time. My brother beat him up first... for taking me out in the first place... then he explained, he said 'look, he's a real idiot, I don't want you hanging around with that sort of people.' I'd still see him around, but I don't bother doing anything with him anymore.*

More common, but more complex and protracted, is where an individual gradually breaks away from dependency on a peer group. In such cases, separating from delinquent peers is likely to stem from some concurrent or preceding transitionary event, such as leaving one's home town or giving up excessive drug and alcohol use. For girls, leaving school in particular presented an opportunity to relinquish ties with delinquent peers and start a new life.

Many of the girls reported having serious problems at school and, as found in the survey, the act of leaving school could change their behaviour dramatically. In many cases, leaving school meant severing ties with school friends who had adversely influenced their behaviour, or provided an opportunity to relinquish a reputation for disruptive behaviour. Leaving school and moving on to some form of employment, training or further education offers an opportunity to form new friendships in a more adult environment.

> *...my friends used to be encouraging as well, saying 'yeah come on, lets go and do this, do that' so I just used to be stupid and go and do it. ...As soon as I went to college it was just different. A different atmosphere, the people were different. The students were different. I think that if I had gone to the same college that all my friends did, then maybe I would have carried on doing the same things. But because I decided that 'I don't want to go with my friends, I want to go and find new friends' I found out exactly which college everyone was going to and I made sure I went to a different one. ...I just thought that I didn't want to be round them any longer than I had to. I was there for school, I wanted to start a new life, knowing that I had no education behind me ...I knew that if I didn't get good*

grades I'd have to work up for the rest of my life, so the best thing to do is move away from my friends, go to college, and I thought that was much better for me. The best move I could ever have done. ...I made more friends and they weren't anything like the ones I left behind at school.

In contrast to leaving school, the potential effects of leaving home on offending behaviour are more uncertain. For some, moving away from a home environment or neighbourhood in which parents, siblings or peers are involved in offending, can also offer a fresh start. But for others, the very act of leaving home may create a whole new set of problems, including attachment to a new group of delinquent peers. In practice leaving home, especially for boys (see Chapter 5), is as likely to escalate as reduce involvement in offending, and will depend on a wide range of factors, not least of which is whether a young person possesses the emotional maturity and the necessary resources to begin to build a life of their own, or is pushed out prematurely into a world of uncertainty, insecurity and risk.

One interviewee described how, on falling out with his mother and leaving home at the age of 16, he was introduced to drugs for the first time and "it just escalated from there". He described how his offending behaviour from then on was inextricably related to drugs, including buying stolen goods in exchange for drugs and threatening clients who owed him money. Experimentation with drugs is often associated with a high risk lifestyle which includes other forms of offending behaviour, even though the age of onset of offending tends, on average, to precede drug use by two to three years.

In Chapter 5, it was shown how continuing involvement in offending is also closely associated with heavy alcohol use, often with friends of the same inclination. The interviews with desisters confirmed these findings. There are ways, however, in which young men can extricate themselves from such a lifestyle. A change may be triggered by some external influence, such as acquiring a stable relationship with a woman, which can help a young man to acquire a sense of manhood in ways which associating with his fellow peers cannot. One interviewee described how he stopped getting into trouble when his partner persuaded him to stop drinking, whilst several referred to how having children led to them stopping drinking and starting to behave more responsibly.

I find that when you have a family your relationships with your friends seem to get pushed to the back a bit. ...I don't just think of me, I am now a family. I don't go out drinking at night, I prefer to drink indoors, I don't go and sit in a pub much. I've lost contact with most of those sort of people [with whom his offending was

associated]. I don't deal [drugs] no more, well, I don't really smoke
[cannabis] no more. I'm slowly pulling away from that circle of
people. Something was holding me back because it was difficult to
pull away from them.

In general, interviewees stated that committing criminal offences was closely related to other forms of problematic or "childish" behaviour, especially alcohol and drug abuse. Interviewees were often unable to distinguish the reasons for giving up these forms of behaviour from the reasons for giving up offending. The regular consumption of alcohol and experimentation with drugs are common features of teenage lifestyles and many of the factors which influence desistance from drug and alcohol abuse will apply equally to offending. Ultimately, it is not clear to what extent desistance from offending precedes, coincides with or follows desistance from alcohol and drug use – all three may well apply in different cases – but for many young people the same influences may well lead to desistance from all three kinds of behaviour.

Adolescence is a period of uncertainty in which identities are tentatively constructed and in which efforts are made to find a sense of direction and achieve a sense of belonging. Close attachments to peers are both a symptom and a product of these pressures, but delinquent peer groups cannot offer long term solutions to them. Thus in addition to finding ways of disengaging from delinquent peer groups, young people must also be offered escape routes in the form of legitimate opportunities for growth and self-development.

Forming stable relationships and having children

The survey findings showed that for females, forming partnerships, getting married and having children were all strong predictors of desistance. (Indeed all of the married women in the sample had desisted from offending.) The interviews clearly confirmed these findings. One interviewee described how her live-in boyfriend had been able to influence her away from getting involved in fights by preventing her from going into town at night. Another described how her relationship with an older man had kept her out of trouble.

I met N-- and my life settled down quite a bit. He was older than
me. ...I wanted somebody who had a sense of direction of where
they wanted to be going. So then my life settled down, and I moved
in with him. ...I felt that I'd found what I'd been looking for, I'd
been searching for something. ...Then he was 23, the age gap
doesn't show now, but then I needed somebody who was a bit older,

who wasn't going to get me into trouble, somebody who was fairly solid and reliable.

But the greatest influence on desistance came not from partners but from having children. All of the mothers interviewed spoke of the profoundly positive influence that children had on their lives, outlook, identity, sense of responsibility and behaviour. Several young women stated that responsibility for children had brought about a complete change in their lifestyle: they drank less, used fewer drugs, socialised less, saw their friends less and stopped offending.

I think its the best thing that's happened to me. Otherwise I'd be an alcoholic. ...That really changes your life when you've got children. ...Before I just used to think of myself all the time but now I think of my children first. You just stop thinking about yourself, going out and enjoying yourself, you want what's best for them.

I'd say that having [a son] was one of the best things that happened to me. Without him I'd probably be dead. Like before I had him when I was working in the pub, you tend to go out every night, and just get totally pissed. You'd just get really bad, its no way to live really. .... I was on a self destruct course basically. There's more to life than going out and getting pissed.

These changes arose out of the practical and emotional consequences of motherhood. Opportunities for offending are severely reduced. Finding babysitters, finance and time to go out is difficult. Having children meant a daily routine, putting your own needs second, becoming responsible for someone else.

The kids [are] the biggest change [since early teenage]. ...They've put some order into my life. A routine. ...Your life is ordered as soon as you have a child, you have to be responsible. You're not just coping with yourself now, there is somebody looking for you for every-thing, and you've got to be there for them.

But having children does not act as an automatic panacea. One interviewee, for example, continued to get involved in fights after her children were born and was still striving to control her violence at the time of the interview. She worried, however, about the consequences of her fighting for her children. There was the risk of getting seriously injured in a fight or the risk of impris-onment if she injured someone.

There's people now when you go down the town who wouldn't think twice getting a glass out now and walloping you, so obvi-

ously you've got to think "I can't get involved in this in case some-thing happens and who's going to look after the kids after that?"

She was also concerned about what the children would think of her if she came home covered in bruises or if they found out that she had a reputation for being a fighter. Another interviewee was similarly concerned about the repercussions her offending might have for her children, even though she didn't yet have any.

One other reason why I stopped was that I know that I want to have children when I'm ready, and I don't want my children growing up knowing that I was that kind of person that used to just go around fighting. I don't want to be a mother that's been fighting all the way through her life and still can't stop even when she's had children. I don't want them to be brought up like that.

An important effect of having children is its influence on an individual's identity and sense of maturity. All the interviewees with children described how they became less self centred and referred to the increase in responsibility which accompanies parenthood. For some, this change in how they perceived themselves arose in part out of a improvement in the way in which they were perceived by their parents.

Before I had kids I was always out with different boys, never in, always out, always getting drunk, ...but when I had my first kid I tried to stop all that. I tried get a home together. I just changed, my whole life just changed. As a person I felt more responsible, I could have stayed going out and having a good time, but I didn't, ...I've got on better with my family since then, they've said I've matured; I'm not sure how I did, but they said I did. I don't regret having children, it was that best thing I ever did.

For young men, the effects of settling down and having children are not so immediate or apparent. Not all the young men who formed new families stopped offending. Half of the male interviewees were married at the time of the interview, or had been in the past, but of these, most had continued to offend for some time after forming a long-term relationship. In some cases relationships exerted a restraining effect during periods when the relationship was good, but any stresses and problems in the relationship led to depression, drinking and offending. For some, the relationships just weren't strong enough to bring about the necessary conditions for desistance. But for others, relationships had a clear and beneficial effect. One interviewee described how a stable relationship at the age of 20, 18 months of which was in marriage, affected his behaviour.

Well, it's women i'n'it... they change your life... That's all that matters to me when I'm in a relationship - the woman. And I tend to stay away from the pubs and all that when I'm with a woman. I remember going into the pub with my wife... I'd been in there the previous two weekends and it had gone off, and the landlord come up to me, and there was a fight in there on this particular night, and I stayed right out of it, I was with me wife; and the next day I went in there and the landlord said to me: 'why don't you bring your wife out every time?' I said 'why?' He said, 'well that's the only time you're never fighting'. So maybe meeting her, you know, stopped it.

As with young women, the overall effect of having children was usually beneficial for young men, at least in retrospect. In the short term, having children tended to come as a considerable shock, increasing levels of stress and sometimes triggering flight from the relationship. Facing up to the responsibilities of fatherhood in practice was often difficult and often took "a long time to get used to". It often depended on their age and their maturity. One interviewee described how, at 21, he was just "too young" for fatherhood.

[Being a dad] was alright ...but I was only with it for 3 months, but yeah it was a good feeling. But things started to go wrong and I moved out then. She was still here for a while. And I used to baby sit on Saturday nights so she could go out with her mates. The baby used to scream the house down, it did my head in, I couldn't wait to leave it.

The findings from the main survey did not extend to young people over the age of 25 and it is suggested in the conclusions to Chapter 5 that young men may begin to grow out of offending *after* the age of 25. The interviews with desisters included one male respondent aged 27 and it is worth noting how, by this age, the influence of children on his life and his sense of responsibility had, with the benefit of hindsight, become of considerable importance.

Probably the single largest change in my life is children. Once you have children you are no longer responsible just for yourself, you're also responsible for somebody else. Somebody else's life, their future too ...and I owe it to my children too, to secure their future.

Several of the older men who had children related the experience to stopping offending. As one father put it:

Its the responsibility of being a father - you've got kids now, you're not the teenager that you used to be. Its an improvement to be settled down now. I have two children and you feel more mature. I

*just want to sit at home and be with me bairns and take them to
the park.*

As found for women, having children can alter a man's self perception and
the way he is perceived by others, especially his family of origin.

*I've got a commitment; I've got the bairns to look after. And they
(his parents) are seeing that; they are seeing me as a more mature
adult; and I think they respect me for it and I respect them.*

Parenthood is the most powerful rite of passage in contemporary society
and, in many cases, is accompanied by acceptance into the world of adulthood. The sense of responsibility engendered by parenthood – gradually
among men and more immediately among women – leads to changes in the
way in which the needs of other people are perceived, which in turn are
linked to cognitive changes which reduce propensities to commit offences.
Having children forces one to think of the consequences of one's own
actions, including criminal actions.

Acquiring a sense of direction

The majority of young people in their late teens and early twenties are
neither married nor have children. More of the young women will begin to
settle down during this period than the young men, but since offending
begins to drop off as early as the mid-teens, there must be other reasons why
some young offenders desist. In addition to establishing a stable relationship
and having children, young people can acquire a degree of maturity by
taking on responsibilities, forging commitments and establishing a daily
routine through structured and meaningful activity. One interviewee
stopped offending when she got involved in religion.

*I just want to try and live my life how the bible says. I really believe
it's true. That's made a really big influence on my life. ...I wouldn't
dream of doing half the things that I used to do. ...I always believed
in God. I didn't really understand anything to do with the bible, so
really for me it was a new discovery. If you read it, it tells you the
things you should be doing and not doing, and really that's the best
way of life. Even if its not true, what they predict, it still makes
somebody a much better person.*

Others found a deeper meaning to their lives through voluntary work. One
young man, for example, found providing cheap furniture to disadvantaged
groups had influenced his behaviour and had shown him there were others
worse off than him.

...this voluntary work I'm doing [has] really done some good. Coz one thing I've realised recently is that no matter how bad you are [financially] there's hundreds of other people out there who are a damn sight worse off than you are.

Employment training schemes could provide a sense of structure and direction and one young woman felt her involvement on a YTS course had stopped her offending.

I was given an opportunity to, by the YTS. It was a lot different from school because it was a lot more disciplined and you couldn't truant or takes days off here there and everywhere. I settled down a lot more... When I knew I was going to do [YTS]; anything criminal I kept well away from because I didn't want to jeopardise that. I had an opportunity to stop before it was too late...

The fear of losing a position as a consequence of offending was echoed in comments about work. One interviewee's primary motivation for avoiding "trouble" was that it would risk him losing his live-in job in a country restaurant, which would also result in homelessness. Another feared losing his job as a consequence of his employer finding out about his involvement in fights.

I had a job. And A___'s a small town, I was working in the local hospital ...you go out on a Friday night and bump into 10 or 20 people you worked with, one of them's only got to see you scrapping or getting up to no good and off they go up the hospital and tell everybody, its just bad news.

For others, it was not just the risk of losing one's job, but also of jeopardising future prospects.

I've got more to lose. I need a good reference from work if I want a decent job and I'm looking for a decent job because I'm looking for a graduate job, so I wouldn't really want to jeopardise that.

Securing employment helped some interviewees stay out of trouble not so much because it provided a legitimate source of income, but because it provided them with a sense of financial responsibility. One man aged 19 described how once he started work, he took over responsibility for earning the money to pay the bills and now did all the paperwork for the family's finances. His family (mother and siblings) now saw him as the main breadwinner. Another began to appreciate the monetary value of things.

Once you start working or paying taxes or things like that, and then you think you're paying for all these services, so when that bus shelter over there gets smashed its tax payer's money. Or the bus fares go up to pay for the glass getting smashed...

Others no longer committed acquisitive offences because, through employment, they had enough money to buy the things they needed. One young woman, for example, shoplifted cosmetics and other consumables in her teens because she could not afford them. Once she had enough money to buy the things she needed, she stopped. However, several interviewees mentioned lapsing back into offending on occasions when they had no money, even after a decision had been taken to stay out of trouble. This illustrates an important point, namely that the process of acquiring and maintaining a sense of direction can be undermined by changes which can, often suddenly, affect people's lives and lead them back into a life of offending. But the above also illustrates that where young people can find a sense of direction, particularly through employment, it may lead to a sufficient investment in, or commitment to legitimate activities which they are unwilling to jeopardise by breaking the law.

Realising in time or learning the hard way

Some feared the physical consequences of their own violent behaviour – either in terms of injury to themselves or injury to other people. One interviewee described how she began to question her involvement in fights as she began to reflect on the consequences of her actions both for herself and for others.

I'm different. I've calmed down... I used to be a bit of a loud mouth. I'm a more quiet person now. I was more childish then. I used to do stupid things. Pick arguments for no reason. As I gradually got older I thought to myself 'why am I fighting? why am I bullying someone else, coz I wouldn't like to be in that situation'. So, from there I did learn from my lessons really, after I got beaten up one time I thought 'why am I doing this?' It stopped me. I thought about it and I thought 'I don't need this'. And I've never had a fight since. ...Before I left school I wasn't scared of violence, but when I got into college I got scared of it and I backed off from it"

For some, their continued involvement in offending led to criminal convictions, whilst others feared they might end up in court or even custody if they didn't stop soon. Leaving school or reaching the age of 16 was perceived as a watershed after which the repercussions for committing offences became serious.

...now I've left school; if you get caught for it you go straight to court now, don't you.

...that all stopped [shoplifting] around the age of 16. Basically 'coz I realised that I was at the age where if I got caught for it I could get done for it. Under 16 it would just be a warning or something, it didn't bother me that much.

The perception that as one gets older warnings stop and real punishment begins was echoed by a number of interviewees. Some saw the threat of imprisonment as a strong deterrent.

If I'd got caught shoplifting every time I did it, yeah, I'd have had cautions for the first two times and the third would have been 'young offenders' [institution].

I think that because I was scared of the police and I was scared of getting picked up and put into jail, the thought of that frightened me and I thought I never want to end up in a jail or in prison or in any thing like that.

Those who had been convicted of offences in the past gradually became aware of the potential repercussions of repeated offending – the implications of having a criminal record, the problem of being labelled, whether offending was "worth it" – before they made conscious decisions to stop.

It was a conscious decision that I had to make. ...As I got older I didn't see the point in what I did, coz at the end I thought "what happens if I get caught? – A criminal record." ...You think of the long term consequences and it just wasn't worth it.

[If you get caught] you're marked down... you are labelled [a thief]. I'd rather not have that kind of label.

The process of desistance tends to occur gradually and often intermittently with earlier attempts to stop offending thwarted by outside pressures or changes in circumstances. For one interviewee, who consciously decided to stop on a number of occasions during his late teens and ultimately "learnt the hard way", a number of influences, and in particular the realisation that offending was wrong and the imminent threat of imprisonment, eventually came together over a three-year period to end his offending career.

Realising that its wrong is the main [reason for stopping]. It's realising that these things don't pay. All of them don't pay... in the long run, anyway. Short-run, they might do a little bit. But then you get

> *caught. Then you get taken to court. Then you keep reoffending,*
> *you keep on getting back to court.. and then that's when they say*
> *right .. borstals, prisons and I mean, I don't want to go to prison, I*
> *don't think I could survive in prison. I know lots of people in*
> *prison – lots of my friends. The impact of the police worked on me.*

For others, it was the experience of imprisonment which deterred them from further offending.

> *It's either live outside or live in prison isn't it. That's the choice*
> *you've got. If you're in between crime and leading a good life,*
> *you're in between living a good life or living a prison life. And I'd*
> *like to live a good life and stay at home. ...[Prison] scared me. It*
> *does, it scares you prison. ....People in prison are nutcases. .... I've*
> *had the experience and I don't want it again. It's not good. I'd just*
> *rather live a normal life and try to stay out of trouble.*

Thus in many cases it is not one specific event or experience which leads to desistance, but some combination of influences which change a person and their lives.

> *I think what it was that [my son] was born. That's what's caused it.*
> *...I think it was the thought of being in prison and I've got a bairn*
> *now and I've got to look after number one. At the moment I've got*
> *no need to go out and do anything. For a while after school I went*
> *off the rails, but I realised that I had a life to lead and that there were*
> *better things than being in prison. I've settled down with kids and it*
> *hit me in the head sort of – 'you've got to sort your life out now'.*

The decision to stop offending was often a rational decision based on an appraisal of the costs and benefits of continuing to offend and in particular the costs of increasingly severe penalties as one gets older. The threat or the fear of imprisonment, the influence of the police and the courts, the realisation of what imprisonment does to one's children or one's friends – all these can contribute to the process of desistance. But to ensure desistance, these experiences have to bring about a cognitive change which ensures that offenders fully realise that crime doesn't pay, that it is morally wrong, that one's actions adversely affect the lives of others and that one has responsibility for people other than oneself.

Maturity, responsibility and moral development

Most interviewees gave concrete reasons for stopping offending. A few said they gradually "realised it was wrong", but most said that it was because they had grown up, calmed down, were less childish, more responsible or mature or simply no longer felt the "need" to offend. Being more mature meant seeing other people's point of view, taking responsibility for others – parents, siblings, partners, children – and ultimately for themselves.

I don't know what it is that puts it behind you. I put it down to the acquisition of responsibility. You've got a responsibility to yourself. You've got a responsibility to people you work with. Your family. And being caught and labelled as a thief can diminish that responsibility.

It meant feeling ashamed of one's actions, whether towards the victim or towards friends or members of the family and thinking about the consequences of your behaviour rather than acting impulsively.

I'm alright giving someone a hiding one night, but I can't stand facing them the next day. I don't like thinking, 'I'm going to bump into that bloke down the high street, oh shit, what am I going to say?'. And this place is so small, its such a small town if someone's hit someone the whole town knows about it the next day. And it just causes too much trouble.

When I was younger I worked on an impulse basis. If I wanted to do something I went out and did it – I didn't even think about the consequences of what I was doing. Up to the age of about 16 or 17. ...Whereas now if I get an idea about something that I want to do I spend a lot more time thinking about how it's going to affect other people around me. ...So I'm a little more sensible.

Acting sensibly, thinking before doing something and respecting others are all hallmarks of maturity. During the transition from childhood to adulthood, various landmarks such as leaving home and forming partnerships are passed, which may act as stimulants or hindrances to the development of maturity. In practice, however, the process of desistance is complex and as this final quotation illustrates, it frequently comprises a combination of a number of influences.

I think the silliness had to stop, like the ultimate thing that the parent dreads is the daughter getting pregnant, and I did that. And once I'd done that I couldn't really rebel because how can you rebel with like a kid?! ...I still don't think that I was grown up during the pregnancy. I think it was after the baby was born... I think it's being on my own... Away from [ex-partner] away from my parents and whatever else. I'm here, if anything gets done it gets done because I do it. I think it's lack of time as well. If you've got a lack of time you can hardly get into trouble.

The life-history interviews have shown that events and experiences associated with desistance exert their effect through bringing about changes in an individual's identity, outlook and sense of maturity and responsibility. Most young offenders who eventually desist from offending do so by disengaging from other delinquent or deviant influences, making a fresh start, finding some sort of direction and meaning in life, settling down and forming a family of their own or by learning that ultimately crime doesn't pay. Whilst on the whole young men up to their mid-twenties are less likely to undergo these changes than young women, there are clearly some individual men who constitute exceptions and it is on the basis of their success that policies for encouraging the more intransigent offenders to give up a life of crime could be developed.

7 Discussion and conclusions

The findings of this national self-report study of offending by young people are largely consistent with other studies of delinquency, both in this country and elsewhere (see, for example, Junger-Tas *et al*, 1994; Farrington, 1994a; Riley and Shaw, 1985; Rutter and Giller, 1983). Like other self-report studies, the findings show that offending amongst young people is widespread and that a substantial proportion of young people are actively engaged in committing a wide range of property and violent offences, from shoplifting, burglary and handling stolen goods to threats, assaults and the consumption of illegal drugs. While most offenders commit no more than one or two offences, a substantial minority admitted to committing more than five offences in 1992 and to using drugs (predominantly cannabis) on a regular basis. Given these prevalence and incidence rates, efforts to prevent or reduce offending and drug use amongst young people must be of paramount importance.

Criminality prevention entails preventing individuals from ever starting to offend and, in the event that they do start to commit crimes, to stop them from offending as soon as possible thereafter. The former can be achieved by developing a range of policies which impact upon the factors which predispose young people towards committing offences. The latter can also be achieved this way, but more often the prevention of reoffending is considered to be the responsibility of the criminal justice system. However, as the Home Affairs Committee on Juvenile Offenders noted (House of Commons 1993), this is a comparatively expensive way to reduce crime. An alternative, which this study begins to illuminate, might be to identify the strongest influences on offending and reoffending during the transition to adulthood in the context of an individual's personal and social development and develop policies which encourage natural processes of desistance and discourage criminogenic influences.[1]

Where offending is spread widely but thinly across a large proportion of the population, the most effective response is likely to be to universally target the onset of offending via a variety of social policies. In this study, nearly half of all 14- to 25-year-olds admitted committing at least one offence at some time in their lives. The majority of these young people commit only one or

---

1   This would be in keeping with the new philosophy of part of the Criminal Justice Act 1991, which introduces the notion of individual maturity into the sentencing of young offenders.

two mostly minor offences and for them, the costly intervention of the criminal justice system should be avoided as far as possible.

However, this study also found that three per cent of offenders accounted for about a quarter of all offences, which is in line with other work which has found that a small minority of offenders are responsible for a disproportionate amount of offending (Home Office, 1993; Hagell and Newburn, 1994). For this high risk group of young offenders, social policies to encourage desistance need to be combined with criminal justice policies aimed at preventing reoffending. The findings presented above (as well as other recent research) confirm that both types of response are necessary, but it was not possible within the confines of this study to assess the effects of formal sanctions on desistance. The main implications for policy are therefore confined to identifying priority areas for intervention and prevention at different stages of development. It is likely, however, that if crime is reduced by improving informal controls, the chances of detection and conviction are likely to increase for the remainder who continue to offend.

In Chapter 4, the main factors which distinguish offenders from non-offenders were identified. Of the demographic, family and school variables included in the analysis of the onset of offending, four factors stood out as strongly correlated with offending – low parental supervision, truancy and exclusion from school, having friends and/or siblings who were in trouble with the police and poor family attachment; 80 per cent of males with all of these risks were also offenders. The findings from the in-depth interviews with desisters in Chapter 6 confirmed the importance of peer, family and school factors as the main influences on starting to offend.

Once young people start to offend, the role of the family and the school diminish, while other influences begin to prevail. Peer influence continues to exert a powerful influence on the behaviour of males (for whom it may become even stronger), and to a lesser extent females, but overall the offending careers of males and females tend to follow quite different paths. Whereas females tend to grow out of offending as they pass a series of landmarks on the way to adulthood, the same pattern is not evident in the case of males.

In Chapter 5, the main factors which were found to be statistically associated with desistance from offending were identified. For females, these comprised leaving home, entering into stable relationships with the opposite sex, forming new families and eventually becoming economically independent, socially responsible and self-reliant individuals. For males, however, none of these factors were found to be statistically associated with desistance. For them the avoidance of, or extrication from a delinquent lifestyle, including drinking heavily and using drugs, is the key precondition for desistance from crime. The findings from Chapter 6, however, suggest that there are events and experiences (external to the criminal justice system) which can influence *individual* young men to stop offending. By building on both sets of findings, the remainder of this chapter explores a number of implications for the development of policy and concludes with some suggestions for future research which builds on the findings of this study.

Preventing the onset of offending

As found by other research on why some young people turn to crime, the quality of family relationships is identified as pivotal to why young people start to commit offences. Those with a poor relationship with one or both parents are more likely to be inadequately supervised by their parents, to truant from school, to associate with other delinquents and ultimately to offend themselves. Young people living with both natural parents were found to be less likely to offend than those living with one parent or in a step family, but these differences are largely explained by differences in the quality of relationships between young people and their parents and the capacity of parents to exercise effective supervision. One of the most important components of any criminality prevention strategy must therefore be to improve the quality of relationships within families and the capacity of parents to effectively supervise their children.

Strengthening families

There are many ways in which families can be strengthened and Utting *et al* (1993), in a detailed review of research on the relationship between families and crime, sets out some of the "ingredients" of family-based crime prevention. They suggest a three tier approach comprising (i) universal services, which would be available to every family and child, (ii) neighbourhood services, which would only be available in areas of high crime and social disadvantage and (iii) preservation services, which would only be available to a small number of families and children who have come to the attention of social services. Some aspects of this approach might be worthy of consideration.

Universal services have the advantage of not stigmatising those who receive them as 'families of potential criminals'. The most important universal service is the provision of training in parenting skills in relation to all the developmental stages of childhood (i.e. from birth through to the teenage years). A national programme of parent education would be expensive, but strengthening families would help to produce multiple benefits, including reductions in child abuse and improvements in mental health, school performance and employment prospects.

Targeting specific neighbourhoods is less expensive and, it could be argued, less stigmatising than targeting families at risk. Open access family centres could become the cornerstone of a neighbourhood-based approach to criminality prevention. They already offer a range of services from family therapy to play groups (sometimes on a self-help basis), and in some cases they may help families stay together by keeping children out of care and helping to prevent abuse, neglect or family breakdown. They also offer a venue for parents who want a place in which to share their experiences and some offer respite for parents undergoing periods of extreme stress at home. Their effectiveness can be enhanced if volunteer outreach workers are used for reaching the most isolated families. Alternatively (or additionally), health visitors might be used to identify families in trouble at an early stage and refer them for assistance to family centres. An example of the former is Home-Start, which uses experienced parents as volunteers to visit the homes of families with pre-school children who are under stress. An evaluation of Home-Start suggests that it is successful in preventing children being taken into care (Gibbons and Thorpe, 1990) and given the strong links between 'care' and 'criminal' careers (see, for example, Walmsley, 1991), this might be an initiative worth developing more widely.

In practice, most family support services are for parents of young children and are not aimed at parents of teenagers. Given that many parents experience great difficulties with their children when they reach adolescence – the average age of onset for other forms of deviant behaviour, such as truancy and running away from home, is also around 13 to 14 – it is perhaps surprising that more support is not available to parents with teenagers. Open access family centres may well offer a spring-board for developing explicit, family-based criminality prevention services, which provide local support for parents with children of all ages, but perhaps a specialised form of support for parents of teenagers could be encouraged, similar to Home-Start and using experienced parents as volunteers. Together with open access family centres to oversee the co-ordination of services for families at risk, this could open up avenues for pursuing family-based crime prevention in a more systematic form than has hitherto been possible.

Preservation services target dysfunctional families who are usually known to the social services and in some cases the police. Efforts to turn such families around, often through the use of therapy and parent training, are necessarily resource intensive. Evaluations of family preservation initiatives in this country and abroad suggest that they can be effective in reducing physical and sexual abuse and preventing children being taken into care. There is also evidence to suggest that family preservation can produce considerable financial savings compared with foster or residential care (Kelly, 1992), although care needs to be taken to ensure they are not stigmatising, particularly if the service targets families other than those already known to the authorities.

Under the Children Act 1989, local authorities have a statutory responsibility to provide services for families and children in need and a duty to take reasonable steps to encourage children not to commit criminal offences. The Department of Health are currently in the process of drawing up a Circular which will require local authorities to assess the need for the provision of services for families and children and to draw up and publish three-year plans. Amongst those whose needs will have to be addressed are young offenders and families in need of support and it may be that the findings of this study and their implications for strengthening families as outlined above could be incorporated into such plans.

Improving parental supervision

The quality of family relationships was also found to be strongly related to how effectively parents are able to supervise their children when away from the home, which in turn is closely associated with truancy, association with delinquent peers and offending. Those who have a poor relationship with one or both parents are likely to spend less time at home, more time in situations which offer opportunities for committing offences and, most importantly, are likely to care less about the consequences of their behaviour for their family. Thus interventions which improve family relationships are also likely to improve parental supervision.

Poor parental supervision may not simply reflect a lack of knowledge as to the whereabouts of one's children or the company they may be keeping, but a lack of interest in where they may be, what they are doing and with whom they spend their spare time. A few parents may even condone the anti-social behaviour of their children outside the home. But the vast majority of parents care about what their children get up to and who they associate with and for them there are also measures which they can take which directly impact upon their capacity to supervise their children outside the home.

Riley and Shaw (1985), in their study of parental supervision and delinquency, suggested a number of pointers for parental action which apply equally today. Parents could be encouraged to accept that poor relationships with their children can have implications which extend beyond the four walls of their homes, that it may be their children who are committing offences (not somebody else's) and if they are, parents should make it clear that they strongly disapprove of such behaviour. They could also be encouraged to clearly point out to their children what may happen if they are caught offending or using drugs, what the effects of offending behaviour may be on the family and the local community and if their children do end up in trouble with the police, remain committed to them and supportive of their needs. Most importantly, as children enter adolescence, parents should recognise and begin to acknowledge their emerging adult status and in doing so, adopt a more co-operative approach to the enforcement of rules and expectations.

One finding of this study is that children from single parent (and step) families are more likely to commit offences than those brought up by two natural parents. This is largely accounted for by the greater likelihood that young people living in single or step families are more likely to have a poor relationship with one or both of their parents (even though the majority will still have good relations with one or both parents). However, a weak association between family type and parental supervision was also identified, which suggests that single parents are hindered from exercising effective supervision simply because they lack the support of a partner or because they (along with step families) tend to be financially worse off than other families. In an earlier study of parental supervision and delinquency, Wilson (1980) found that the most socially disadvantaged mothers (including single mothers) tended to exert the least supervision. Single parents and step families therefore require special forms of support if they are to exercise the same degree of supervision over their children as two parents particularly, in the case of single parents, where they spend much of their time away from the home at work.

Whilst family-based interventions are necessary for effective prevention, they are not sufficient. As children grow older, the effects of a poor relationship with a parent and lax parental supervision can be compounded by adverse experiences at school and since it is known that interventions which focus exclusively on one particular arena (e.g. the home) or one actor (the child or the parent) do not appear to be effective in the long term (Kazdin, 1985), it would seem that an effective criminality prevention strategy must also extend into areas outside the family. In this study, both truancy and exclusions from school were found to be directly related to offending, indicating that schools are also of primary importance in preventing criminality, particularly since they play such an important mediating role in the development of delinquent peer groups (Reid, 1993).

Strengthening schools

As with offending, truancy is strongly related to poor relationships with a parent or parents and low levels of parental supervision. However, truancy is also independently related to offending (as is exclusions from school and, for females, low school attachment), which suggests that schools themselves may play a part in promoting or reducing propensities to offend. This concurs with the findings of other research, particularly on school effectiveness, which has found that disruptive behaviour and persistent non-attendance are strongly related to the organisation and ethos of individual schools, irrespective of the kinds of pupils who attend the school (see Graham, 1992; Mortimore *et al*, 1988; Rutter, 1979). Effective schools offer their pupils a sense of achievement irrespective of ability, encourage commitment and full participation in all activities, integrate pupils of all abilities and backgrounds, provide clear and consistently enforced rules and promote good relations between pupils and their teachers. In contrast, ineffective schools tend to categorise pupils who behave badly or persistently truant as deviants, inadequates or failures and shift responsibility for the behaviour and welfare of difficult pupils to outside agencies or institutions (Graham, 1992).

There have been a number of government led initiatives in the last few years in the field of education which are likely to impact upon levels of crime and delinquency. In 1989, the Elton Committee of Inquiry into discipline in schools (DES, 1989) summarised those aspects of school management which head teachers need to consider in efforts to improve the effectiveness of their schools. Recently issued government circulars and guidance on pupil behaviour and discipline (DfE, 1994a) and school attendance (DfE, 1991 and 1994c) now encourage the 'whole school' approach to behaviour, attendance and discipline. Schools which adopt the principles of the whole school approach should, therefore, be making a direct contribution to the prevention of criminality through improvements in behaviour and attendance. But it is more recent government initiatives on reducing truancy and exclusions from school which may be particularly likely to impact on criminality.

Reducing truancy

The DfE, through its grants for Education Support and Training, funded over 80 projects for reducing truancy in 1993-94. The projects are designed to improve attendance levels at designated schools and identify and disseminate good practice. Some projects involve parents, others focus on improving the technology of registration, whilst still others are concerned with the relationship between truancy and exclusions or truancy and bullying. Further projects are being funded under the current GEST programme for truancy and disaffected pupils.

A number of measures have also been introduced for reducing truancy nationwide, including the provision of league tables setting out authorised and unauthorised absenteeism rates for individual schools and using computers to improve the administration of registration. The findings of this study suggest, however, that the role of parents is important and whilst the recent circular on school attendance acknowledges the role of parents, it does not specify their responsibilities in any detail.

Where evidence of persistent absenteeism begins to accumulate, it is important that parents are contacted sooner rather than later and any difficulties or problems at home or at school dealt with promptly. In some cases, individual truants may benefit from counselling, in other cases it may be preferable to involve the whole family. Since truancy is associated with low levels of parental supervision, efforts to improve contact between parents and the school should be encouraged.

Research on truancy has found that children who truant at primary school or begin to build up a reputation for persistent absenteeism during the first year of secondary school, are more likely to be excluded from school at some later date for disruptive behaviour or persistent non-attendance (MVA Consultancy, 1991). The transition from primary to secondary school, which is recognised as an important transition in the lives of children, offers an opportunity to ensure that a child with a reputation for truancy (or poor behaviour at school) gets a new start. The importance of this needs to be recognised, since reputations carried over from primary school do little to help children settle to the new and more demanding environment of secondary school. Other measures which can be (and are) taken to reduce truancy range from truancy sweeps to home visits by education welfare officers, but the findings here suggest that whatever the approach, parents must be involved and, where possible, explicitly informed not only of their responsibility for their child's attendance at school, but also of the wider repercussions of them not doing so.

Reducing school exclusions

Like other research, this study found that not only are truancy and exclusions from school strongly associated with offending, but also that they are strongly related to each other. Many of the above measures for reducing truancy will also have a positive impact on the behaviour of pupils at school, but there are specific measures which schools can adopt for reducing exclusions. Recent education legislation requires schools to publish attainment and attendance records, introduce a National Curriculum and standard assessment tests. These changes may exert pressures on individual schools which inadvertently result in a rise in the number of pupils excluded from mainstream education.

In 1992, a survey of exclusions (DfE, 1992) found that the numbers of pupils being excluded from school were not insubstantial and a more recent national survey of pupils out of school (DfE, 1995) has confirmed that the number of permanent exclusions from school has been rising in recent years. The number of permanent exclusions recorded for 1993/94 in 101 out of 109 Local Education Authorities (LEAs) was over 10,000. This represents an almost threefold increase since 1991/92. However, it is not yet clear what effect measures taken in the Education Act 1993 (implemented 1 September 1994) and the accompanying guidance in DfE Circular 10/94 (DfE, 1994b) has had on that trend. Given the implications of rising numbers of exclusions for the criminal justice system,[2] it is important to ensure that the provisions of Circular 10/94 (DfE 1994b) are taken up and implemented in practice. The new legislation emphasises that permanent exclusion is to be used sparingly and as a last resort and schools may now no longer exclude pupils indefinitely. However, the national survey of pupils out of school (DfE 1995) found that for over half of the 101 LEAs covered by the survey, the new policy on exclusions has yet to be finalised and approved. The DFEE will begin to collect data on permanent exclusions from individual schools from January 1996.

In addition to the recommendations contained in Circular 10/94 (DfE, 1994b), there are other measures which can help schools continue working with their most difficult pupils. School support teams (teams of peripatetic teachers and child psychologists) avoid the stigmatisation associated with segregation from mainstream schooling and enable responsibility for disruptive behaviour and persistent non-attendance to remain with the school. Most importantly, they allow both pupils and teachers to resolve difficulties within the context in which they arose, utilising, for example, mediation, pupil councils and bully courts to resolve disputes. The national survey of LEAs found that almost all LEAs now have a team with a role in supporting schools with behaviourally challenging pupils, but only five out of 101 LEAs reported doing any formal preventive work.

There will always be a need to permanently exclude a small minority of highly disruptive or disaffected pupils from mainstream education. In these circumstances it is important, as the new legislation emphasises, to ensure that adequate alternative education outside school is made available. Currently, only about a quarter of secondary pupils (and 40 per cent of primary pupils) excluded from mainstream schooling receive home tuition and over half of those who receive such tuition get less than five hours per week (DfE, 1995). The new legislation also places a duty on LEAs to reintegrate pupils back into mainstream education. The national survey found that only 15 per cent of those permanently excluded from secondary schools (27 per cent of primary pupils) are returned to mainstream schooling. There is clearly still some way to go before the new

---

2 Research has found that excluded pupils are more likely to be prosecuted for committing the same offence as those who are not excluded and two and a half times more likely to be incarcerated for the same offence as those who have not (Martin *et al*, 1981; Parker *et al*, 1989).

legislation becomes effective in reducing the chances of pupils out of school from drifting into crime.

Family:school partnerships

To maximise the development of social, cognitive and educational skills in children a model of continuous intervention, from pre-school through to secondary school, incorporating *both* families and schools, is required (Graham and Utting, 1994). To this end, close inter-dependent links could be developed and sustained between families and schools. In practice, however, families and schools tend to socialise children in isolation from one another. Family and school norms and values sometimes conflict and teachers may blame parents for the behaviour of their pupils whilst parents may condone their child's absenteeism. Some schools feel unsupported by parents who, in turn, feel indifference or antipathy towards schools. As found by Mortimore *et al* (1988), an important barrier to improving parent:teacher collaboration is apathy on the part of parents and resistance on the part of teachers.

If parents and teachers, through greater collaboration, were able to improve the academic performance, behaviour and attendance of children in school and the quality of relationships at home, there ought to be a pay off in terms of criminality prevention. The National Survey of Health and Development found that parental interest in their child's education is the most important factor in determining academic achievement at school (Douglas, 1964). Other research has shown that persistent absenteeism is related to parental attitudes to school and parental levels of education (MVA Consultancy, 1991) and where teachers and parents adopt similar approaches to interacting with children, academic performance is enhanced (Hansen, 1986). Since there is also a close association between academic failure and persistent absenteeism, parents should be informed as soon as possible of early indications of non-attendance or a sudden decline in academic performance.

There may be considerable scope for integrating parents more in school life. They can be involved in the induction of pupils transferring from primary school, which has been found to reduce the incidence of truancy in the first year of secondary school (DES, 1989); they can be involved, through home:school agreements, in improving the supervision and control of children who are truanting or behaving disruptively at school or elsewhere; they can form social networks in schools to help balance the influences of adolescent peer groups (Lindstrom, 1993); they can inform teachers of sudden adverse changes in family circumstances brought on by, for example, unemployment, homelessness, family breakdown, serious illness or bereavement; and together with teachers they can learn how best to jointly respond to the emerging needs of adolescents as they grow towards adulthood. Teachers, for their part, can communicate regularly and on a personal basis to parents on positive, not just negative matters relating to their child's performance at school; they can make home visits to build up trust and good relations with parents as a basis for developing a joint approach towards the education and upbringing of a child; and they can strive to construct a consistent approach to discipline and behaviour between the home and the school, ensuring that problems experienced by children are defined and responded to by parents and teachers in the same way.

Since the earlier children start to offend the more likely that they will continue to offend into adulthood, policies designed to prevent the onset of offending should target children before they reach the average age of onset of offending, that is age 13 or 14. It is during these years that delinquent peer groups begin to form and when parents and teachers should be most encouraged to exercise effective control and supervision on young adolescents. However, it is often those families in greatest adversity which are least well equipped to help children become responsible, mature, law-abiding citizens. They often lack access to informal support networks and feel alienated from local service providers. In such circumstances schools, particularly primary schools, may represent the most important, or even the only formal point of contact with the community in which they live. In such communities, it is all the more important that schools do not insulate themselves from the neighbourhood in which they are situated, but aspire to become its central focus.

In 1990, the Home Office published guidance on the partnership approach in crime prevention (Home Office, 1990). It provides examples of community-based partnerships which have been developed to tackle crime and the fear of crime, but explicitly excludes detailed coverage of what it refers to as the separate question of how to prevent young people from embarking on criminal careers. The partnership approach to criminality prevention has yet to be developed, but it could begin with family:school partnerships, which need not, of course, be restricted to preventing criminality but could encompass a wide range of objectives.

The findings presented here suggest that both families and school have a central part to play in preventing criminality, particularly if they could be encouraged to work more closely together. The next section discusses how policies might be developed to encourage desistance from offending for those who have already begun to offend.

Encouraging desistance from offending

In common with other research, this study has shown that offending begins in the early teens, often with expressive property crimes such as arson and vandalism, before moving on to more serious forms of crime, including violent crime and the misuse of drugs. But where it diverges somewhat from other work is in its findings that young men, in contrast to young women, tend not to desist from offending in their late teens and twenties. The prevalence of offending by females in their early twenties is five times lower than among female juveniles, but amongst males (and against expectations) the prevalence of offending actually increases from about 1 in 4 to nearly 1 in 3. This is accounted for by an increase in the prevalence of male involvement in property offending and in particular fraud and theft from the workplace.

This increase in prevalence amongst males is partly offset by a greater rate of decline in the *number* of offences committed by active offenders compared with females. Whereas the average number of offences committed by this group declines between the early teens and the early twenties from five to three for females, the decline for males is greater – from 11 to four. Thus while it would seem that girls do indeed "grow out of crime", the situation for males is somewhat different. Since the number of offences per male offender declines, but the number of male offenders actually increases slightly in the 18 to 25 year age group, it would appear that while some young men grow out of crime, others do not whilst still others grow into it. Additionally, it would appear that some young men may switch away from more visible and risky forms of offending (presumably, as new and less risky opportunities for committing offences present themselves) and towards offences with lower detection rates as they grow older. This would account for the different picture presented by officially recorded convictions, which show an unequivocal decline in offending by males after the age of 18. Thus as young men grow older, some of them "learn" how to avoid being caught rather than how to behave within the constraints of the law. But why they choose to behave differently to young women needs some explanation.

The key to answering this question would seem to be embedded within the different conditions, opportunities and constraints experienced by males and females during the transition from childhood to adulthood. In Chapter 5, it was demonstrated that young males are less likely than females to acquire the means for making a successful transition to adulthood. They are less likely than females to leave home, enter into stable relationships with the opposite sex, form new families and eventually become economically independent, socially responsible and self-reliant individuals. For females, all these factors were found to be important predictors of desistance from offending. For males, however, they were not. Some males will of course not have experienced these events, but for those who do, it would seem that they either have a different effect (e.g. the experience of having children), or that their effects are delayed beyond the age of 25. Alternatively, the effects of such events may be more than offset or undermined by other, more powerful influences which sustain involvement in offending, at least until the mid twenties.

The only factors which seemed to predict desistance for males were found to be, firstly, their perception that their school work was above average and, secondly, continuing to live at home. The protective effect of standard of school work supplies unequivocal evidence to support the contention that schools matter. A detailed assessment of the literature on the effects of schools on delinquency concluded that delinquency is partially contingent upon rejecting or being rejected by school (Graham, 1988). This study has also found that those who regularly truant (i.e. rejecting) or who are excluded from school (i.e. rejected) are likely to offend, but found no association between standard of school work and onset of offending. But since self-assessed standard of school work is a predictor of desistance, this suggests that, as found by Elliott and Voss (1974), it is how schools respond to low performance, and in particular whether the response leads the pupil into regularly truanting or becoming disruptive in school, which is crucial.

Those who, by the age of 21, were still living with their parents were more likely to desist than those who had left home. For these young males, the enjoyment of relatively good relationships with their parents is likely to be a key factor in their decision to remain at home, where they may still be subject to some degree of parental control and supervision. Research by Warr (1993) and Riley and Shaw (1985) has shown that reducing the amount of time teenagers spend with delinquent friends can be accomplished through spending more time with parents at home; it is, apparently, not just a question of the quantity of time spent at home, but also the quality. It would not, however, be appropriate to encourage young offenders to stay at home (even if it was feasible to do so) on the grounds that they would be more likely to desist from offending. The decision and the timing of leaving home is influenced by many factors and some young people will always leave home (or be pushed out of their home) without adequate preparation.

Preparing young people for leaving home

As shown above, the process of transition from one state of interdependency to another is less direct and more drawn out for young males than for young females and whilst leaving home is likely to encourage desistance for females, it is more likely to postpone it for males. In effect, males are detached from the main institutions of social control for longer than females as they drift in and out of casual relationships and casual employment and attach themselves more firmly and more permanently to groups of like-minded peers.

These findings suggest that many young males would benefit from some form of adult supervision, even after they have left home. Parents should be encouraged to accept that their responsibilities towards their children do not abruptly terminate when they leave home, but merely change to reflect a new set of circumstances. Of course the parents of children who have left home will no longer be in a position to directly supervise them, but they can maintain close and regular contact and continue to exert an influence by exhortation rather than command. At the point at which young people leave home, some parents could be encouraged to learn how to parent their children (sons) 'at a distance'.

Ideally young people, once they have left home, should possess the internal controls which render the existence of external controls superfluous. In practice, external controls will continue to be necessary for many but as Braithwaite (1989) has eloquently argued, social control exercised by significant others, particularly the family, is much more effective. As teenagers move from the more controlled environment of their home to the less controlled environment of the community, the need for other sources of informal social control nevertheless becomes apparent. The efforts of parents could therefore be supplemented by encouraging other responsible adults in the community (neighbours, local employees, other parents etc.) to accept a greater degree of responsibility for the supervision and control of young people in public places and for adult men in particular to engage with and provide role models for young males.

The Youth Service, and particularly detached youth workers, could be usefully employed to co-ordinate efforts in the community to increase informal social control. Detached youth workers are uniquely placed in that they work with groups rather than individuals in their natural environment (usually the street). In some cases, they are the only adults able to reach and establish a basis of trust and mutual respect with groups of young people. They can therefore act as intermediaries between young people on the streets and their families and schools, and could form partnerships with them to prevent crime and foster desistance. In France, detached youth workers are commonly used in crime prevention initiatives and the DFEE is currently funding a number of youth work approaches to diverting young people at risk from drifting into crime.

Young people today are less likely to find employment and are less likely to be able to afford independent accommodation than was the case some twenty years ago (Killeen, 1992). As a consequence, young people are under more pressure to remain at home for longer and find it more difficult to contemplate starting a family of their own. Indeed the proportion of young men aged 20 to 24 who were married in 1971 (37 per cent) had declined by more than half by 1987 (15 per cent).[3] These factors are of course inter-related – unemployment constrains income which in turn affects access to independent housing and

---

3   Part of this decline is accounted for by an increase in the number of people co-habiting.

delays leaving home, marriage and forming a family of one's own – but together they form a potent barrier to the attainment of personal and economic independence and establishing an adult identity. Under such circumstances, the peer group takes on a more important and more enduring dimension as the principal (if not the only) source of security, status, sense of belonging and identity. Since, as described in Chapter 6, disassociation from delinquent peer groups is a necessary precondition for desistance from offending, then providing alternative sources of security, identity and direction, especially for those who will leave home whatever the circumstances they are confronted with in the outside world, is of paramount importance.

One of the principal mechanisms for providing a sense of direction and security and bestowing the status of manhood upon young males has traditionally been through the world of work. The experience of work has considerable significance in structuring an identity through providing the social and cultural capital necessary for successfully making the transition to adulthood. If education and training are associated with dependency and work with independency, then it is perhaps not surprising that young men are finding it more difficult and/or taking longer to make the transition to adulthood. But with the declining number of young people in employment, the capacity for the world of work to provide a rite of passage for young males has diminished. Anderson (1990), quoted in Hagan (1994), notes that while factory jobs in the manufacturing sector once promoted a toughness of demeanour among young males, such attributes are a disability in the new jobs of the service economy. It may be that other ways need to be found of making provision for, and publicly acclaiming the status of, adulthood in general and manhood in particular since, as Wallace (1987) proclaims, young men who fail to get work are at risk of drifting into a kind of perpetual adolescence.

Whilst for most young males perpetual adolescence is not the norm, it would seem that the period of adolescence has been extended as a consequence of economic and social changes over the last few decades (Leffert and Petersen, 1995; Chisholm and Hurrelman, 1995). One response to this by the government has been the setting up of the foyer pilot study. Based on the French system of 450 foyers, which provide accommodation and training/employment support to some 45,000 young people aged 16 to 25, it represents an attempt to provide a stepping stone to self-sufficiency for single homeless young people without a steady income. Funded by the DE, the DoE and the Housing Corporation, the British foyers offer, in addition to accommodation linked to training and employment services, training in literacy, numeracy, life skills and independent living. The pilot scheme is currently being evaluated by the University of York.

A variation on the foyer initiative, the Crescent, has been set up by the Surrey Care Trust for young single people who are homeless, unemployed and at risk of offending. The main aim of the initiative is to offer 16- to 25-year-olds who fall into this category of risk temporary shared accommodation, employment training, recreational activities, counselling and support so that they can eventually lead fully self-sufficient and independent lives. Each tenant has to sign up to a contract which not only specifies the details of their tenancy, but also the necessity to abide by "house rules". It is however important to recognise that initiatives such as these are still in their infancy and as yet untested. Care should be taken to ensure that expectations are not unduly raised and it may be prudent to heed some of the criticisms of foyers (see, for example, Gilchrist and Jeffs, 1995). Nevertheless, foyers have the potential to be an important source of attachment for young single people without housing and employment whilst simultaneously providing an environment in which a degree of control and supervision can be developed and maintained.

Initiatives such as these can offer a start to young people leaving home who have little, if any, means for supporting themselves. Most young people who leave home will, however, be attached either to an educational institution, some form of training scheme or an employer. For young females, the sense of direction and/or the access to a legitimate source of income will foster desistance from offending, but for males it does not appear to be sufficient. As illustrated in Chapter 6, acquiring work can offer a sense of direction and personal identity to rival that of the peer group, but for males, it did not predict desistance from offending – at least not on its own. (Indeed, access to work would seem to provide new opportunities for offending which, for some, will undermine rather than encourage desistance.) The next section moves on to the second main stage of the transition from childhood to adulthood – the forming of a new family.

Supporting the forming of new families

The full transition from childhood to adulthood is signified most powerfully and completely in the formation of a new family. The interviews with desisters in Chapter 6 confirm that having children provides an important rite of passage and constitutes a potent influence on desistance from offending. Whilst the arrival of parenthood signifies a major change in the lives of both males and females, the actual responsibilities of parenthood were much more likely to be accepted by females, leading to an abrupt ending to delinquent activities, including the excessive use of alcohol and drugs. For males, however, the sudden arrival of fatherhood can provide the trigger for moving away from the peer group and developing a sense of parental responsibility, but it can also push some into fleeing from their relationship with their partner and withdrawing further into their peer-groups and its associated activities.

For those young men for whom parenthood comes too early, there would appear to be a need for initiatives which assist them to come to terms with the extent and nature of the abrupt change in their personal circumstances and responsibilities. They need induction into their new role as a father, confirmation of the importance of their contribution during the early years of child-rearing and support with the range of bewildering problems which characterise childbirth and the pre-school years. Unlike young mothers, for whom the act of giving birth is a powerful confirmation of their identity as an adult woman, young fathers have no equivalent source of confirmation of their status as an adult man.

The importance of preparation for fatherhood cannot be underestimated. In addition to pre- and post-natal induction courses, fathers could also be reminded of the crucial role they play during their child's teenage years and there may be scope for developing training and support for fathers of teenage children. Poor relationships with fathers was found to be more prevalent amongst offenders than poor relationships with mothers and since young males who continue to live at home are more likely to desist from offending than those who do not (and poor relationships with fathers will mitigate *against* this), the quality of relationships between fathers and sons is likely to be a crucial factor in encouraging desistance from offending. Since fathers generally constitute the principal role model for their sons, there will be inter-generational benefits from improving father:son relationships; good parenting begets good parenting.

Reducing the risks during adolescence

A stark, if somewhat discouraging finding from this study is the fact that many young male offenders are offending well into their mid-twenties (albeit at a reduced rate), and, if they become involved in regular drug and alcohol misuse, their chances of desisting by their mid-twenties are decidedly remote. Once committed to this kind of lifestyle, there are few opportunities or incentives to desist from such behaviour during the transition to adulthood.

A recently published government consultation document on tackling drugs provides evidence to suggest that a considerable amount of drug misuse is financed by crime and recommends a range of actions to help young people resist taking drugs, including more positive role models and the development of skills for reducing peer pressure (Central Drugs Coordination Unit, 1994). The findings here suggest that there is clearly a point in the offending careers of young males when intervention to prevent moving on to drug misuse is both possible and desirable. Since the age of onset of drug use is approximately three years after the age of onset for offending, there would appear to be some benefit in specifically targeting drug prevention initiatives on young offenders aged no more than 13 or 14. These are children who are otherwise likely to get caught up in a sub-culture of peer-led deviant activities which is self-reinforcing and hard to break.

The involvement of young men in heavy drinking, whilst nothing new, also inhibits desistance from offending and, like drug misuse, can deepen a commitment to a delinquent group of peers. Tuck (1989), in a study of drinking and disorder, confirmed that drinking constituted a routine social habit among the young and found that incidents of disorderly behaviour were frequently associated with groups of "bored youngsters with nowhere to go who have drunk too much and are looking for entertainment". She outlines a number of predominantly situational measures for reducing alcohol misuse amongst the young (e.g. avoiding the congestion of entertainment outlets, staggering pub closing times and improving supervision at specific entertainment outlets). But these essentially "situational" measures are unlikely to impact upon the propensity of individuals and groups of young men to indulge in heavy drinking and to use the same as a form of rite of passage.

In the interviews with desisters in Chapter 6, desisters were unable to distinguish between the reasons for giving up drinking or drug use from giving up offending. Other research has consistently identified the same set of antecedents for alcohol and drug misuse as delinquency (Dryfoos, 1990). The coincidence of common predictors for these three types of behaviour suggest that interventions should focus more on the predictors of the behaviour than the behaviour itself. Since many successful programmes of prevention share common elements, it may be worth exploring the possibility of devising a programme of intervention which avoids duplication of effort and funding and co-ordinates preventive services for young people at risk at the local level.

Persistence in offending was not only predicted by alcohol and drug misuse, but also by living or socialising with other offenders, especially siblings, partners (or ex-partners) or friends. Offenders who had recently been victims of violence were also more likely to continue offending as were those who had committed more than just a small number of offences. Braithwaite (1989) suggests that the more commonplace offending is or becomes in a young person's life, the greater the risk that they will become embedded in criminal networks and alienated from legitimate social and employment networks. In Chapter 6, interviews with desisters illustrated how disengaging from delinquent peers is a necessary, but not sufficient prerequisite for desistance. To facilitate disengagement from a delinquent peer group, young offenders could be offered opportunities for involvement in conventional activities and, in some cases, a chance to make a fresh start. Quality employment, as discussed above, offers one such opportunity; others include training, further education, volunteering and involvement in cultural, religious or sporting and leisure activities.

Harnessing informal to formal sources of social control

In the interviews with desisters, criminal and penal sanctions arose as important deterrents to future offending. Fear of causing serious injury, of being caught, of acquiring a criminal record, of losing a job, of being labelled and of ending up in prison, all contributed to a gradual realisation of the full costs of continued offending. The criminal justice system clearly has a central role to play in encouraging desistance. However, the fact that more (or at least as many) young men commit offences in their twenties as in their teens suggests that young men may continue to fear being caught but not enough to stop their involvement in less visible forms of property crime. The development of cognitive skills plays little part in any moral reassessment of the rights and wrongs of property crime, as evidenced by the increase in fraud and theft from the workplace. This suggests that something may be missing, that alongside the fear there is a lack of any moral dimension, a lack of conscience.

Braithwaite (1990) states that one of the most fundamental problems in modern western societies is that as children mature in the family, control by punishment is gradually replaced by a reasoned appeal to internal control, at the core of which is the self-regulating and powerful mechanism of 'conscience'. He goes on to suggest that criminal behaviour is best deterred by developing consciences and that the people best placed to do this are those who mean the most (significant others) to the offender in question. In Chapter 6, young men referred to the importance of the effects of their offending on those closest to them and these attachments have considerable value in promoting desistance. These are the people who can shame future criminality and by doing so can help reduce the attractiveness of peer groups that provide social support and moral legitimacy for crime.

The implication from this is that families, schools and neighbours constitute the most potent forms of informal social control and that to be effective and efficient, the criminal justice system could be encouraged to do more to harness these more potent influences. Given the widespread involvement of young people in crime and drug misuse, the criminal justice system cannot hope to provide all the answers. It needs to be reinforced by, if not subordinated to, the power of significant others to exert effective social control. Supervision orders with requirements for reparation and mediation and cautioning plus schemes constitute examples of existing attempts to widen the scope of criminal justice sanctions, but in neither case are parents centrally involved. One innovative approach which locates parents at the centre of proceedings is Family Group Conferences (FGCs) in New Zealand (see Brown and McElrea, 1994).

Based on the principle of putting the needs of the victim and his/her family uppermost and restoring relations between the victim and the offender to one of parity, FGCs place families at the centre of the decision making process and thus ensure they take responsibility for their young people. This underlying principle is based on the idea that the natural development of mutual rights and obligations in families provides a foundation for the development of the same in wider social relationships, which in turn are seen as a necessary (if not sufficient) condition for preventing reoffending.

In practice, the FGC, which is affiliated to the Youth Court, is attended by the young offender, members of the family (in the wider sense), the victim, an advocate for the young offender (if requested), a police officer and a social worker. The family can also request the attendance of anyone else, such as a teacher, an employer, a representative of the community or a voluntary organisation. Decisions in the form of action plans are ratified by the Youth Court, which acts as a back stop if the plans break down or are patently inappropriate. Sanctions available to the FGC include reparation, formal apologies, community work and, most importantly, undertakings to attend school or not to associate with co-offenders. Thus two of the most important correlates of offending – truancy and association with delinquent peers – are directly incorporated in the response to offending and the central part played by families – the other most powerful influence on offending – institutionalises the power of family attachments to induce a sense of shame, atonement and responsibility. Family Group Conferences are already being piloted in the child care field. An evaluation currently being undertaken at the University of Southampton will hopefully provide some insight firstly into whether FGCs could work in this country and secondly whether they could be adapted to the prevailing circumstances in the youth justice system.

This study of young people and crime has shown that families, schools and peer groups constitute the powerful influences on the behaviour of young people as they progress towards adulthood. It has also shown that for young male offenders, there are few options which seem to unequivocally encourage desistance. Staying on at home helps some, resisting drug and alcohol misuse helps others, but on the whole there are few mechanisms of control outside the criminal justice system which affect their lives once they leave home. Whilst living in this vacuum of social control young men, in contrast to young women, are also further restricted by a lack of appropriate opportunities for achieving maturity and a sense of social responsibility. There are few incentives for relinquishing attachment to the one predictable source of security they have – their peer group. And if it is a delinquent peer group, there will be few incentives to relinquish attachment to a life of crime. It is in this context that the criminal justice system needs support from other sources of control and supervision.

Some future directions for research

Given what is now known about the factors which influence the onset of offending, the role of research may be to focus more on assessing and evaluating innovative prevention programmes rather than conducting more empirical research. The above discussion of the implications of this study's findings for policy and practice has included a number of practical suggestions, such as the French system of foyers and Family Group Conferences from New Zealand, which could be developed and evaluated on an experimental basis in this country. Indeed the Home Office Programme Development Unit has been set up with this explicit purpose in mind. However, far less is known about what influences desistance from offending and here further empirical research would be beneficial.

Firstly, there is a need to explore further the finding that most young males do not grow out of crime before their mid-twenties. It may be that they grow out of crime *after* the age of 25 – in which case it would be useful to know why – or it may be that they merely switch to offences with lower detection rates, such as fraud and theft from the workplace. To what extent is this a conscious decision to seek out less risky offending opportunities or merely a reflection of the fact that entering the world of work presents new possibilities for committing offences? It would also be useful to know more about the characteristics of those who are committing fraud and theft from the workplace in their twenties, and in particular whether they are different from other offenders in terms of their background, their motives and their attitude towards breaking the law.

Secondly, given the important influence of parental supervision and family relationships (particularly between fathers and sons) on the onset of offending, there must be scope for exploring in more depth the kind of parenting (and especially fathering) which not only constitutes good practice in terms of preventing onset, but also constitutes the most effective response to promoting desistance from offending. How can parents help their children (particularly their sons) to disengage from delinquent peers, refrain from misusing drugs and protect them from ultimately becoming locked into a criminal lifestyle? What can they do to prepare them for leaving home and how can they exercise a degree of control over their lives once they have left home? What role, if any, can schools play in supporting parents in this and how could family:school partnerships be constructed in such a way as to further such aims?

The Department of Health has recently announced a five-year programme of research into how formal and informal support can be mobilised to help parenting. Its focus is on situations which put stress on parenting and the prevention of parental breakdown and its main aim is to discover, through research, effective solutions to the problems of parents in stressful environments. The programme will encourage research on specific parenting problems, such as parental neglect and indifference and how parents cope with adolescents at risk of, or in trouble with, the law. And it will also support research into links between informal and formal support networks. Some of the questions posed above could be addressed by research commissioned as part of this programme.

Finally, and perhaps most importantly, this study begs the question as to what role the criminal justice system plays in promoting (or perhaps inhibiting) desistance. The findings of this study have shown that the transition from childhood to adulthood is fraught with difficulties and that whilst some young people (particularly females) acquire the attributions of adulthood during this transitionary period, some do not. Age would seem to be a very poor proxy for maturity and yet the criminal justice system defines all those over the age of 17 as adults and is restricted to sentencing them accordingly. In Germany, judges possess the discretionary power to sentence young adults (those aged 18 to 21) according to either adult law or to the more flexible juvenile law, with its much wider range of sanctions. Young adult offenders are only sentenced under adult law if the judge assesses their maturity as being equivalent to that of an adult. In practice, the proportion of young adult offenders sentenced as adults has been steadily declining since 1970 and today the vast majority of young adults who commit criminal offences in Germany are sentenced as juveniles (Graham, 1990). Whilst there has been some work on the effectiveness of the criminal justice system in deterring further offending, there has been very little, if any, empirical research on how the criminal justice system links into and either reinforces or undermines the potentially positive effects of various transitions in the period from childhood to adulthood. Perhaps research into how the sentencing of young adults could be made to reinforce naturally occurring opportunities for desisting from offending would reap benefits in terms of reducing the number of young offenders who graduate to a life of crime.

Appendix A. Survey design and methods

Questionnaire and data collection method

The questionnaire comprises questions on social and demographic factors, self-reported drug use and offending. It is based on a standard instrument developed for the International self-report delinquency study (ISRD) by the Dutch Ministry of Justice, but differs in a few important respects (Junger-Tas *et al*, 1994). It includes a wide range of background factors on respondents' lifestyles and covers additional offences such as cheque and credit card fraud, insurance, tax and benefit fraud and serious motoring offences (see Appendix B).

A number of changes were made to the wording of questions about offending in order to reflect more accurately the definitions of criminal offences in England and Wales. For example, to the question, "did you ever take away a car?" was added "...without the owner's permission", making the question unambiguously a criminal offence. Similarly, the question "did you ever set fire on purpose to something not belonging to you" was amended to read "...on purpose or recklessly...", bringing the question in line with the precise definition of arson. In order to avoid the inclusion of very minor thefts, questions about stealing from school, home or work were limited to those where what was taken was "worth more than £5".

Questions on socio-demographic factors was conducted face-to-face and lasted about half an hour. Next, a booklet of questions on the use and sale of controlled drugs was completed by the respondent and placed in an envelope. This was followed by a self-completion booklet comprising a list of offences numbered one to 33. The respondent was asked to read out the number corresponding to the offence admitted and a self-completion booklet for each one was handed to the respondent. All the booklets were placed in an envelope and sealed to ensure complete confidentiality. The entire questionnaire lasted, on average, just under one hour.

Self-completion was chosen for the self-reported offending section to ensure confidentiality and to minimise the risk of concealment or exaggeration. These advantages, however, were partly offset by the fact that the interviewer was unable to check whether the respondent had completed every question. As a consequence, the level of non-completion in the drugs and offending self-completion booklets was higher than it might have been.

Piloting

The questionnaire and sampling method were piloted in October 1992 in the city of Birmingham. Thirty-seven interviews were achieved, after which full debriefing sessions with the interviewers were held and the question-naire redrafted before the main stage of the fieldwork commenced.

Sampling

Three samples were generated – a national random sample, a random sample in areas of high victimisation and a booster sample of ethnic minorities. Each of the three samples was generated by selecting households at random using the Post Office's Postcode Address File (PAF).

This "pre-selected random sample" tightly controls any selection effect by giving interviewers as little choice as possible over who to interview. Clearly, however, the sampling frame employed does not include a number of people not living in households such as students, nurses, the homeless and those in residential care, Young Offenders Institutions and prisons. Although the most frequent and serious offenders are likely to be in the last two of these groups, they are estimated to comprise no more than one-quarter of one per cent of the target population. It seems unlikely, therefore, that the inclusion of these groups would influence the number of individuals committing offences, although their inclusion might have increased the average frequency of offending, particularly for serious offences.

Screening and response rates

A total of 32,121 addresses were screened, of which 3,856 (12%) were found to contain a young person aged 14 to 25. Since some postal addresses contain more than one household it was necessary to screen each address for multiple households and select one at random. Invalid addresses (e.g. businesses premises, vacant, derelict or demolished premises) were filtered out by the interviewers. Of the 3,856 eligible addresses, 166 were ineligible for one reason or another (e.g. the respon-dent was ill or away from home) leaving a sample of 3,690 households containing one or more eligible respondents. If there was more than one person in the target age range living at the address, the interviewer selected one at random to be interviewed. A total of 2,529 interviews were completed with 14- to 25-year-olds, representing an overall response rate of 69 per cent.[1]

The national random sample comprised 893 respondents and the random sample in areas of high victimisation 828 respondents giving a nationally representative sample of 1,721 (after weighting). The ethnic minority booster sample, used only to make comparisons among different ethnic groups, comprised an additional 808 cases giving a total sample size of 2,529.

Fieldwork

Fieldwork was carried out by MORI, a private sector survey company, from November 1992 to January 1993. One hundred and fifty-five interviewers were employed to conduct the survey fieldwork. Almost all (99%) of the interviews took place at the home of the respondent. Fifty-four per cent of interviews were conducted alone, 11 per cent with someone else present for part of the time and 36 per cent with others present for the duration of the interview. In only five per cent of the interviews did the interviewer believe that the presence of others had definitely affected the interview. Twenty per cent of respondents required help with the self-completion booklets.

Sample representativeness

The sample was compared with other data sources to ensure that it was broadly representative of the general population. A comparison between the age and sex breakdown of the National Population Census and the survey's core sample indicated that younger respondents were somewhat over-represented and older respondents correspondingly under-represented. Compared with data from the Labour Force Survey, students and unemployed people and those on youth training schemes were over-represented in the sample. This skew in the sample was broadly similar across ethnic minority groups.

From interviewers' ratings of how well the contact address was maintained, it appears that non-respondents were rather more likely than respondents to live in very poorly maintained dwellings in poor and vandalised neighbourhoods. Thus, the sample is slightly biased against respondents living in poorer localities.

---

1 Refusals – on the part of either the respondent or their parents – accounted for just over half of those households where an interview was not conducted and non-contacts accounted for the rest. Among those aged 14 to 21 who agreed to be interviewed, about four per cent refused or otherwise failed to complete the drugs booklet and/or the booklet on offending. The estimated response rate for this part of the survey was, therefore, approximately just over 64 per cent.

On each of the dimensions examined, the extent of the differences between the *core sample* and the characteristics of the general population are small. Some differences were found between the ethnic minority booster sample and the general population when broken down by age and sex, and by employment status and sex. Given the sample sizes for comparison, however, this is not surprising. The sample of ethnic minorities was also markedly skewed towards respondents living in areas of high ethnic minority concentration as a result of the sampling method used; in order efficiently to sample ethnic minorities from pre-selected addresses, it was necessary to use as primary sampling units, enumeration districts which contained a minimum of 10 per cent of the relevant population.[2]

Weighting

Weights were calculated to correct for unequal selection probabilities. These comprised a "household weight" to up-weight cases where more than one household was identified at an address (and which would otherwise be under-represented in the sample); and an "individual weight" which up-weighted respondents selected in households with more than one young person. These two weights in combination make the national sample representative of young people in the population. A third weight was used in order to analyse the national and high crime samples together. This down-weighted the high crime sample and up-weighted the random sample.

---

2   Eighty-two per cent of the primary sampling units selected for the Afro-Caribbean sample, 98 per cent of those for the Indian sample, 60 per cent of those for the Bangladeshi sample and 83 per cent for the Pakistani sample were drawn from racially mixed inner metropolitan areas.

Appendix B. List of criminal offences included

Expressive property offences

1. Damaged or destroyed, on purpose or recklessly, something belonging to somebody else (for example, telephone box, bus shelter, car, window of a house, etc.).

2 Set fire on purpose or recklessly to something not belonging to you. It might be to paper or furniture, to a barn, a car, a forest, a basement, a building or something else.

Acquisitive property offences

3 Stolen money from a gas or electricity meter, public telephone, vending machine, video game or fruit machine.

4 Stolen anything from a shop, supermarket, or department store.

5 Stolen anything in school worth more than £5.

6 Stolen anything from the place where you work worth more than £5.

7 Taken away a bicycle without the owner's permission.

8 Taken away a motorcycle or moped without the owner's permission.

9* Taken away a car without the owner's permission.

10 Stolen anything out of or from a car.

11 Pickpocketed anything from anybody.

12* Snatched from a person a purse, bag or something else.

13* Sneaked or broken into a private garden, a house or a building intending to steal something (not meaning abandoned or ruined buildings).

14 Stolen anything worth more than £5, not mentioned already (for example, from a hospital, youth club, sports centre, pub, building site, etc.).

15 Bought, sold or held onto something you knew or believed at the time had been stolen.

16 Sold a cheque book, credit card, cash point card (ATM card) belonging to you or someone else so that they could steal money from a bank account.

17 Used a cheque book, credit card, cash point card (ATM card) which you knew or believed at the time had been stolen to get money out of a bank account.

18 Claimed on an insurance policy, an expenses form, a tax return or a social security benefit form that you knew to be incorrect in order to make money.

Violent offences

19* Threatened somebody with a weapon or with beating them up, in order to get money or other valuables from them.

20* Participated in fighting or disorder in a group in a public place (for example,   football ground, railway station, music festival, riot, demonstration, or just in the streets).

21* Beaten up someone not belonging to your immediate family, to such an extent that you think or know that medical help or a doctor was needed.

22* Beaten up someone belonging to your immediate family, to such an extent that you think or know that medical help or a doctor was needed.

23* Hurt someone with a knife, stick or other weapon.

*Analysis of onset and desistance based on those who admitted three or more of the offences listed or one offence marked (*)

Appendix C. Supplementary tables: individual offences

Table C1
Cumulative participation in offending by sex

Offence	all	males	females	sex ratio	
	%	%	%	%	
Vandalism	9.4	14.2	4.5	3.5	****
Theft from phone etc.	3.5	3.6	3.4	1.1	
Shoplifting	19.7	23.9	15.5	1.7	****
Theft from school	5.3	7.2	3.3	2.3	***
Theft from work	6.4	11.4	1.5	8.4	****
Bicycle theft	4.9	7.7	2.1	3.9	****
Motorbike theft	1.8	3.3	0.2	13.6	****
Car theft	2.0	3.4	0.6	5.9	***
Theft from car	2.8	4.6	1.1	4.4	****
Pickpocketing	0.9	1.3	0.5	3.0	
Snatch bag	0.3	0.5	0.1	3.1	
Burglary	3.1	5.5	0.7	7.9	****
Theft from other	2.5	4.3	0.8	5.7	****
Handling	20.2	26.4	14.1	2.2	****
Sold cheque book	0.5	0.6	0.4	1.6	
Used stolen book	1.1	1.7	0.6	2.7	
Fraud	5.0	8.5	1.4	6.6	****
Threat for money	1.4	1.9	0.9	2.2	
Fighting	16.0	23.9	8.1	3.5	****
Arson	3.9	5.8	2.0	3.1	***
Beat non-family	4.4	7.7	1.1	7.2	****
Beat family member	1.4	2.1	0.7	3.1	*
Hurt with weapon	4.3	6.5	2.2	3.1	***
Unweighted N	1,684	738	910		

Table C2
Current participation in offending by sex

Offence	all	males	females	sex ratio	
	%	%	%	%	
Vandalism	2.6	3.7	1.6	2.3	*
Theft from phone etc.	0.9	0.7	1.3	0.5	
Shoplifting	3.4	4.5	2.4	1.9	*
Theft from school	1.1	1.1	1.1	1.0	
Theft from work	1.8	3.4	0.2	15.9	****
Bicycle theft	0.5	0.9	0.1	7.3	
Motorbike theft	0.3	0.5	0.0	20.6	
Car theft	0.9	1.5	0.2	6.5	*
Theft from car	0.5	0.8	0.3	3.0	
Pickpocketing	0.2	0.5	0.0	–	
Snatch bag	0.1	0.2	0.0	6.7	
Burglary	1.2	2.4	0.1	16.2	***
Theft from other	0.5	1.1	0.0	42.7	*
Handling	9.7	12.5	7.0	1.9	***
Sold cheque book	0.1	0.1	0.0	1.5	
Used stolen book	0.5	0.8	0.2	4.6	
Fraud	2.8	5.5	0.1	44.6	****
Threat for money	0.3	0.6	0.1	5.4	
Fighting	5.0	6.7	3.3	2.1	**
Arson	0.9	1.3	0.6	2.2	
Beat non-family	1.3	2.0	0.5	4.3	*
Beat family member	0.2	0.4	0.0	16.2	
Hurt with weapon	1.1	1.8	0.5	3.9	*
Unweighted N	1,538	676	862		

Table C3
Cumulative male participation in offending, by ethnic origin

Offence	White ↓	Black	Indian ↓	Pakistani	Bangladeshi ↓	
	%	%	%	%	%	
Vandalism	15	4	5	10	<1	****
Theft from phone etc.	4	5	3	3	0	n.s.
Shoplifting	25	22	20	19	0	***
Theft from school	6	14	16	6	0	****
Theft from work	12	3	<1	2	1	****
Bicycle theft	8	12	3	8	0	*
Motorbike theft	4	0	0	2	0	n.s.
Car theft	4	1	2	8	3	n.s.
Theft from car	4	3	5	4	3	n.s.
Pickpocketing	1	1	1	1	0	n.s.
Snatch bag	1	0	0	0	0	n.s.
Burglary	5	2	4	4	5	n.s.
Theft from other	5	3	4	5	0	n.s.
Handling	27	18	25	25	13	n.s.
Sold cheque book	1	3	<1	2	0	n.s.
Used stolen book	2	0	3	3	0	n.s.
Fraud	8	1	2	1	0	****
Threat for money	2	0	1	3	0	n.s.
Fighting	24	21	16	21	12	**
Arson	6	8	1	5	5	n.s.
Beat non-family	8	6	3	6	5	n.s.
Beat family member	2	0	1	3	0	n.s.
Hurt with weapon	6	1	5	9	8	n.s.
Unweighted N	675	86	114	119	46	

All samples (including booster sample); weighted percentages
"Other Asian" and "other" ethnic groups were excluded from this analysis.
n.s.= non significant *p<.05 **p<.0.01 ***p<0.001 ****p<0.0001

Table C4
Cumulative female participation in offending, by ethnic origin

Offence	White ↓	Black	Indian ↓	Pakistani	Bangladeshi ↓	
	%	%	%	%	%	
Vandalism	5	2	2	0	0	n.s.
Theft from phone	4	3	1	0	0	n.s.
Shoplifting	16	25	13	1	1	****
Theft from school	4	4	1	<1	1	n.s.
Theft from work	2	3	0	0	0	n.s.
Bicycle theft	2	3	0	0	2	n.s.
Motorbike theft	<1	0	0	0	0	n.s.
Car theft	1	0	0	0	0	n.s.
Theft from car	1	0	0	1	<1	n.s.
Pickpocketing	<1	2	3	0	<1	n.s.
Snatch bag	<1	0	1	0	0	**
Burglary	1	4	0	0	0	*
Theft from other	1	4	0	<1	4	***
Handling	14	21	6	3	2	****
Sold cheque book	<1	0	0	0	0	n.s.
Used stolen book	1	2	0	0	0	n.s.
Fraud	2	2	0	0	0	n.s.
Threat for money	1	3	0	1	0	n.s.
Fighting	9	19	2	6	0	***
Arson	2	4	1	0	0	n.s.
Beat non-family	1	3	0	0	0	n.s.
Beat family member	1	0	0	0	2	n.s.
Hurt with weapon	2	5	1	1	0	*
Unweighted N	825	116	94	86	58	

All samples (including booster sample); weighted percentages
"Other Asian" and "other" ethnic groups were excluded from this analysis.
n.s.= non significant *p<.05 **p<.0.01 ***p<0.001 ****p<0.0001

Table C5
Cumulative participation in drug use by ethnic origin and sex

1) Males

Drug	White ↓	Black	Indian ↓	Pakistani	Bangladeshi ↓	
	%	%	%	%	%	
Cannabis	42	23	28	10	9	****
Heroin	1	<1	1	3	0	
Methadone	2	3	2	0	1	
Cocaine	4	2	2	3	0	
Crack	1	2	5	2	0	****
Ecstasy	10	4	1	1	0	****
Acid/LSD	12	3	12	3	4	****
Tranquillizers	1	0	1	0	0	*
Amphetamines	12	<1	16	0	0	****
Temazepam	1	0	1	0	0	****
Magic M'rm	12	6	10	2	0	***
Glue/Gas	5	1	0	4	0	
Any drug	46	24	29	12	10	****
Unweighted N †	683	88	114	119	48	

2) Females

Drug	White ↓	Black	Indian ↓	Pakistani	Bangladeshi ↓	
	%	%	%	%	%	
Cannabis	26	22	4	9	2	****
Heroin	<1	0	0	0	0	
Methadone	<1	3	4	7	0	**
Cocaine	2	1	0	1	0	
Crack	1	1	0	0	0	
Ecstasy	5	2	1	0	0	**
Acid/Lsd	8	2	0	0	0	****
Tranquillizers	1	1	0	0	0	
Amphetamines	7	0	0	0	0	***
Temazepam	1	0	0	0	0	
Angel Dust	<1	0	0	0	0	
Magic M'rm.	5	0	0	0	0	**
Glue/Gas	4	2	1	0	0	
Any drug	27	25	7	16	2	
Unweighted N	828	116	95	88	58	

*p<.05 **p<.0.01 ***p<0.001 ****p<0.0001
All samples (including booster sample); weighted percentages
"Other Asian" and "other" ethnic groups were excluded from this analysis.

Table C6
Current participation in offending by age-group

Offence	Males				Females			
	14–17 %	18–21 %	22–25 %		14–17 %	18–21 %	22–25 %	
Vandalism	3.3	6.4	–	**	3.9	0.3	–	***
Theft from phone etc.	1.2	0.3	0.2	n.s.	1.6	1.7	0.1	n.s.
Shoplifting	3.2	8.1	1.0	***	5.3	0.6	0.3	***
Theft from school	2.9	–	–	***	2.6	–	0.1	**
Theft from work	0.6	2.9	8.2	****	0.4	0.1	–	n.s.
Bicycle theft	2.1	–	0.4	*	0.2	0.1	–	n.s.
Motorbike theft	1.2	–	0.2	n.s.	0.1	–	–	n.s.
Car theft	1.0	0.9	3.3	n.s.	0.6	–	–	n.s.
Theft from car	0.9	1.1	0.2	n.s.	0.7	–	–	n.s.
Pickpocketing	–	1.1	0.2	n.s.	–	–	–	–
Snatch bag	0.4	–	–	n.s.	0.1	–	–	n.s.
Burglary	5.0	1.1	0.4	**	0.3	0.1	–	n.s.
Theft (other)	1.8	0.5	0.7	n.s.	–	0.1	–	n.s.
Handling	11.2	17.9	6.8	**	8.9	7.5	3.0	*
Sold cheque book	–	0.2	–	n.s.	0.1	0.1	–	n.s.
Used stolen book	1.1	0.9	0.2	n.s.	0.2	0.1	0.3	n.s.
Fraud	0.1	5.2	13.7	****	0.2	0.1	0.1	n.s.
Threat for money	0.5	1.1	–	n.s.	0.2	–	0.1	n.s.
Fighting	9.8	6.8	1.7	**	4.9	3.8	0.2	*
Arson	2.2	1.2	–	n.s.	1.5	–	–	*
Beat non-family	2.8	1.2	2.0	n.s.	1.2	0.1	–	n.s.
Beat family member	0.5	0.5	0.2	n.s.	0.1	–	–	n.s.
Hurt with weapons	3.3	1.2	0.2	*	1.1	–	0.1	n.s.
Unweighted N	276	227	173		303	284	275	

n.s.= non significant *p<.05 **p<.0.01 ***p<0.001 ****p<0.0001
Core sample, weighted percentages

Appendix D. Multivariate analysis

Logistic regression is a multivariate statistical technique used to measure the strength of the relationships between an independent or predictor variable (e.g. having delinquent peers) and a dependent or outcome variable (e.g. offending) once possible associations with other variables have been taken into account. Central to this method are estimations of the increase or decrease in the chances of an event occurring (e.g. offending or desistance from offending) that are associated with each social or demographic factor examined. This change in risk may be expressed statistically as an odds ratio. This expresses the odds[1] that an event will occur in one condition (e.g. offending among those who have delinquent peers) relative to the odds that an event will occur in the absence of that condition (e.g. offending among those who do not have delinquent peers).[2] If the odds ratio is equal to 1, there is no association; positive values indicate a corresponding increase in odds; negative values indicate a corresponding decrease in odds. This statistic therefore expresses the increased or decreased probability of starting or stopping offending given the presence of a specific risk or protective factor.

Logistic regression is designed for data where the dependent (or outcome) variable takes a binary form (for example offender vs. non-offender; desister vs. persister). It makes assumptions about the form of the relationship between the dependent and independent variables: namely, that there is an additive relationship between the logarithm of the odds of an event occurring and the set of independent factors. This can be expressed as:

$$\log (\text{odds (event occurs)}) = \text{constant} + \beta_1 x_1 + \beta_2 x_2 + ... + \beta_n x_{1n} + \text{error term}$$

---

1   Odds are another way of expressing information on probability. Where probability=p, odds = p/1-p. For example if the probability that something will occur is 50% (or 0.5) the odds that it will occur are 0.5/1-0.5, which equals 1. Similarly, if p=0.25 odds=0.3 and if p=.75 odds=3.

2   For example, the probability of offending among males who have delinquent peers is 0.7 (70%), and the odds of offending among this group are thus 2.3. The probability of offending among those who do not have delinquent peers is 0.35 (35%), and their odds of offending (0.54). The ratio between these two odds (2.3/0.54) is equal to 4.3. It may be concluded from this calculation that (before accounting for other factors) having friends in trouble with the police increases four-fold the odds of offending among males. The odds ratio (the natural antilogarithm of the β-coefficient) presented in the logistic regression tables, is analogous. Thus it can be seen that the increased odds of offending among males who have delinquent peers is 3.7, after taking account of other risk and protective factors.

$\beta_1...\beta_n$ indicate a set of 'n' coefficients (estimated in the modelling); $x_1....x_n$ indicate a set of 'n' independent factors. The latter are often in the form of indicator variables: for example x_f may indicate whether or not someone knew other people who were in trouble with the police ("delinquent peers") – so the coefficient β_f only contributes to the odds among those who did have delinquent peers. Positive values of β_f would indicate that the odds of starting to offend and later continuing to offend are higher for those who have delinquent peers; negative values that they were lower. The interest lies in those factors with β values significantly different from zero. The test can be based on the Wald statistic which has a chi-square distribution.[3]

A statistic that is used to look at the strength of association between the dependent variable and each of the independent variables is the "partial correlation" labelled in the tables as the R statistic.[4] R can range in value from -1 to +1. A positive value indicates that as the variable increases in value so does the likelihood of the event occurring. If R is negative the opposite is true. Small values for R indicate that the variable has a small partial contribution to the model.

In addition to estimating the relative importance of a number of variables relative to one another, logistic regression also allows an estimation of the overall impact of a model – or set of variables taken together. This form of analysis fits a model to the data which maximises the amount of variation explained in the dependent variable (onset or desistance) by including in the model those factors which produce the largest reductions in unexplained variation. The "model Chi-squared" provides an estimate of the amount of variation explained by the model.

Modelling onset of offending

Chapter 4 examines the extent to which starting to offend may be explained by family relationships, school experiences and peer-group relationships after allowing for the effects of other possible influences. The findings from the bivariate association between each factor and offending are summarised in Table D1.

The next step in the analysis was to construct a model containing all the onset variables (see Tables 4.1, 4.2 and 4.3) and then delete one by one those factors which, allowing for the influence of other variables, do not add anything to an explanation of starting to offend (a procedure known as backwards stepwise deletion). Tables 4.4 and 4.5 in Chapter 4 show the variables which remained in the model of onset of offending for males and females respectively.

---

3 When a variable has a single degree of freedom, the Wald statistics is just the square of the ratio of the coefficient to its standard error. For categorical variables the Wald statistics has degrees of freedom equal to one less than the number of categories.

4 This statistic is directly analogous to the correlation coefficient Pearson's *R*, except that it takes into account the effects of other relevant variables.

Table D1
Change in odds of offending (bivariate)

Factor	Change in odds of ever offending‡			
	Males		Females	
Strongly attached to family	-3.2	****	-2.3	****
Close parental supervision	-2.3	****	-2.7	****
Siblings in trouble with the police	2.4	**	5.9	****
Strong attachment to school	1.0	n.s.	-2.4	****
Above average school work	1.0	n.s.	-1.5	n.s
Truanted from school	3.4	****	3.1	****
Temporarily excluded from school	3.7	****	3.7	***
Permanently excluded from school	61.5†	***	6.2	**
Friends in trouble with the police	4.3	****	4.2	****
Unweighted N	632		801	

n.s.=non-significant *p<.05 **p<.0.01 ***p<0.001 ****p<0.0001
†The magnitude of the increased probability of offending among those permanently excluded from school arose because a very large proportion of this group (98 per cent, n=17) had committed a criminal offence.
‡ a minus sign indicates a decreased odds of offending

Onset of offending among males

From Table 4.4, it can be seen that delinquent peers and truancy from school are the most robust (i.e. statistically significant) correlates of starting to offend (p<0.0001) and that, even after controlling for other relevant influences, these factors increase the odds of offending by a factor of 3.7 and 2.5, respectively. Weak supervision and having siblings in trouble with the police were significant at the level of p<0.01 while exclusions from school approached statistical significance (p<0.1) controlling for other influences. The column showing the change in odds of offending among those having the characteristic mentioned takes account of the influence of the other factors included in the model. The partial .correlation coefficient shown in the column marked R indicates that after controlling for other factors, peer delinquency has the strongest correlation with offending (R= 0.2). The model performed well, explaining a large and statistically significant amount of scaled deviance (model chi squared=118, (5 d.f.) p<0.0001).

Onset of offending among females

For females, it can be seen from Table 4.5 that having friends in trouble with the police is the most robust correlate of offending (p<0.0001) and that, after controlling for other factors, this increases the odds of offending by a factor of 5.6. Parental supervision and truancy from school were also strongly correlated with offending (p<0.001), both of which increased the odds of offending by a factor of two. Strong attachment to family was significant at the five per cent level and attachment to school was statistically significant at the 10 per cent level, after controlling for the influence of other relevant factors. This model also performed well (model chi squared=125, (5 d.f.) p<0.0001).

Modelling intervening variables

As discussed in Chapter 4, two of the strongest correlates of offending – truancy and association with delinquent peers – are similar forms of behaviour to offending itself and need themselves to be explained. To this end, further multivariate analysis was conducted, modelling firstly truancy and then association with delinquent peers. The results are presented in Tables D2 to D5.

Table D2
Truancy: final model (males)

Variable	β	s.s.	odds ratio	R
Social class‡		†		0.04
IIINM	0.33	n.s.	1.4	0.00
IIIM	0.77	**	2.2	0.08
IV/V	0.56	†	1.7	0.04
Family structure§		**		0.12
Single-parent family	1.00	***	2.7	0.12
Step family	0.53	n.s.	1.7	0.03
Strong attachment to family	-0.94	***	-2.6	-0.11
Close parental supervision	-0.88	****	-2.4	-0.14
Siblings in trouble	0.62	†	1.9	0.04
Peers in trouble	0.81	****	2.3	0.14
Standard of school work	-0.55	†	1.7	-0.77

†p<0.1 *p<0.05 **p<.0.01 ***p<0.001 ****p<0.0001
core sample, unweighted data
499 cases included in final model
‡Estimate of the increased odds of truancy for the social classes shown are compared with classes I&II
§Estimates of the increased odds of truancy for those brought up in the families shown are compared with those who grew up with two natural parents.

Table D3
Truancy : final model (females)

Variable	β	s.s.	odds ratio	R
Social class‡		†		0.08
IIINM	0.18	n.s.	1.2	0.00
IIIM	0.02	n.s.	1.0	0.00
IV/V	0.69	**	2.0	0.08
Strong attachment to family	-1.01	****	-2.8	-0.15
Close parental supervision	-0.87	****	-2.4	-0.15
Siblings in trouble	1.01	**	2.8	0.10
Peers in trouble	0.42	†	1.5	0.03
Attachment to school	-0.68	**	2.0	0.11

†p<0.1 *p<0.05 **p<.01 ***p<0.001 ****p<0.0001
Core sample. Unweighted data
603 cases included in final model
‡Estimate of the increased odds of truancy for the social classes shown are compared with classes I&II

Table D4
Delinquent peers: final model (males)

Variable	β	s.s.	odds ratio	R
Family structure§		*		0.06
Single-parent family	0.29	n.s.	1.3	0.00
Step family	0.77	*	2.2	0.08
Small family	0.46	†	1.6	0.04
Strong attachment to family	-0.56	*	1.8	-0.07
Close parental supervision	-0.71	**	2.0	-2.00

†p<0.1 *p<0.05 **p<.01 ***p<0.001 ****p<0.0001
Core sample. Unweighted data
499 cases included in final model
§Estimates of the increased odds of truancy for those brought up in the families shown are compared with those who grew up with two natural parents.

Table D5
Delinquent peers: final model (females)

Variable	β	s.s.	odds ratio	R
Family structure§		*		0.07
Single-parent family	0.06	n.s.	1.1	0.00
Step family	0.93	**	2.5	0.09
Close parental supervision	-0.59	**	-1.8	-0.93
Attachment to school	-0.47	*	-1.5	-0.06

†p<0.1 *p<0.05 **p<.01 ***p<0.001 ****p<0.0001
Core sample. Unweighted data
603 cases included in final model
§Estimates of the increased probability of truancy for those brought up in the families shown are compared with those who grew up with two natural parents.

Modelling desistance from offending

Chapter 5 examined the extent to which desistance from offending can be explained by the personal and social development of an individual during the transition to adulthood after controlling for other factors (chronological age in particular). Table 5.2 in Chapter 5 summarised the findings from the bivariate analysis. The second stage involved modelling the social development factors with the data on whether or not respondents desisted or persisted with offending. From Table D6, which shows the findings for males, it can be seen that the odds of desisting from offending for those over the age of 20 were about twice those of their younger counterparts (p<0.05). (The same analysis using age categorised into single-year, 3-year and 4-year age categories indicated that, broadly speaking, the likelihood of desisting increases with age.) After age, the only other social development variable to remain in the model was continuing to live at home with parents, which increases the odds of desistance by a factor of just under two. This approaches statistical significance after controlling for the effects of age (p<0.1). This model of desistance did not perform very well (model chi-square=6.1 (2 d.f.) p<0.05). For males, leaving full-time education, being in work, economic independence, marriage, having children and taking responsibility for self and others were all eliminated from the model.

Table D6
Model of social development and desistance from offending (males)

Variable	β	odds ratio	R
Lives with parents	0.60†	1.82	0.06
Aged 20 or over	-0.66*	1.95	0.10

†p<0.1 *p<0.05 **p<.0.01 ***p<0.001 ****p<0.0001
Core sample, unweighted data
232 cases included in final model

For females the model, using the same set of variables, produced different results (see Table D7). Among females, those who had completed education, were economically independent and living with a partner were significantly more likely than those who had not made these life-transitions to have desisted from offending. In particular, the odds of desisting of those who were living with a partner were more than seven times those of their counterparts, after taking account of other factors. The partial correlation for this variable is also high (R=0.2). Once these factors are taken account of, other transitions such as being in work, leaving home and looking after children and taking responsibility for self and others had only a negligible effect on the likelihood of desistance among females. Once the effect of these variables had been taken into account, chronological age was no longer a relevant variable. This model performed well (model chi square=26.23 (3 d.f.) p<0.0001).

Table D7
Model of social development and desistance from offending (females)

Variable	β	odds ratio	R
Completed education	0.79*	2.21	0.10
Economically independent	0.81†	2.24	0.07
Lives with a partner	2.03**	7.59	0.19

†p<0.1 *p<0.05 **p<.01 ***p<0.001 ****p<0.0001
Core sample. Unweighted data
154 cases included in final model

Explaining desistance using the correlates of onset

The next step was to examine the extent to which desistance from offending could be explained by those factors which were strongly associated with the onset of offending. This analysis indicated that, for males, the odds of *persisting to offend* of those who had friends in trouble with the police were about three times greater than those who did not have friends in trouble with the police. Similarly, the odds of desisting for those who assessed themselves as having an above average standard of school work were about three times greater than those who did not consider their standard of school work to be above average (Table D8). This model performed adequately but left a great deal of variance to be explained.

Table D8
Model of desistance using correlates of onset (males)

Variable	β	odds ratio	R
Friends in trouble with the police	-1.05**	-2.9	-0.19
Standard of school work	1.03**	2.8	0.17

†p<0.1 *p<0.05 **p<.01 ***p<0.001 ****p<0.0001
Core sample. Unweighted data
174 cases included in final model

When the model of onset was applied to the female sample only one variable – exclusions from school – approached statistical significance (p=0.17). This indicates that for females, those factors which are strong influences on starting to offend bear little relationship to the likelihood of desistance. The resulting model was non-significant.

Risk factors and persistence with offending

Since those family and school variables which explain the onset of offending do not adequately explain desistance among males, while remaining at home, performing well at school and having no delinquent peers do, it seemed likely that there would be a number of factors coming into play after onset which sustain a deviant lifestyle. The final stage in the modelling process was to examine the survey data (using bivariate cross-tabulation) to explore whether there were any further variables which were correlated with desistance. The significant factors are summarised in Table 5.3 in Chapter 5. The risk factors were then combined with the social development factors and the correlates of onset to produce a final model of desistance for males and females, as presented in Table 5.4 in Chapter 5 (males) and Table D9 below (females). Both models performed well – for males, the model chi-square=42 (7d.f.) p<0.00005 and for females the model chi-square=37 (3d.f.) p<0.000051.

Table D9
Final model of desistance (females)

Variable	β	odds ratio	R
Completed education	1.16**	3.17	0.16
Lives with a partner	1.71*	5.56	0.15
Committed 5 offences or fewer	1.50***	4.50	0.24

135 cases in final model
*p<.05 **p<.0.01 ***p<0.001 ****p<0.0001
a negative value for the odds ratio indicates a decreased probability of desistance

Appendix E. The effects of age on desistance

The analysis of the correlates of desistance found that for males, chronological age remains an important correlate, even after the life changes that occur during adolescence and young adulthood are taken into account. For females, however, once the effects of social development have been taken into account, chronological age appeared to have no additional explanatory power. This finding was examined by analysing the relative importance of age and social development variables in five stages.

(i) Firstly, using the logistic regression procedure a *model including only age* was created. Chronological age alone accounted for a large amount of variance (sig.<0.0002). This was expected since it is clear that most females rapidly give up offending once they reach adulthood (see Chapter 3).

(ii) Whilst keeping age in the model, further variables were introduced until the model had no additional significant explanatory power. The formation of partnerships entered the model and was more closely correlated with desistance than chronological age. These two variables taken together explain a great deal of the difference between desisters and non-desisters (overall model Chi-Squared= 11.5 (2d.f.) p<0.0007). Because age is *forced* into the model the effects of any life-changes that are closely age-related (such as leaving full-time education) are obscured by its inclusion.

(iii) In order to test the independent power of age as an explanatory variable and test its importance relative to other factors, a model was constructed using *backwards deletion*. The first step of this procedure is to produce a complete model in which the relative importance of each indicator of social development (see Table D4.1) is shown in the form of a logistic coefficient, the statistical significance of which can be estimated. This indicated that age was relatively weak ($\beta=0.84$, p<0.09). The next step of this procedure is to remove each factor one at a time from this over-saturated model until the exclusion of a variable reduced the power of the model to a significant degree. Using this method age was deleted at the sixth step, reducing the model chi squared by only 0.5 (non-significant p=0.48). The resulting model included leaving full-time education, becoming economically independent and forming partnerships (Table D4.3).

(iv) The same result was achieved using a *forward step wise procedure* in which factors were added into the model until no additional variance was explained (overall model Chi-Square=37.5, (3d.f.) p<0.00001). This model based on social development performed substantially better than that including only age and partnerships.

(v) Finally, this conclusion was confirmed by *forcing age into the model last*. In this analysis, chronological age explained only minimal variance once the selected indicators of social development were controlled for (non significant p<0.6).

These findings indicate that once social development is accounted for – in particular, leaving full-time education and forming a stable partnership – chronological age is no longer a relevant explanatory factor. This suggests that some factor (or set of factors) that are closely related to chronological age – e.g. cognitive development, biological maturity or duration of experiences – must account for desistance from offending among males as well as females and not that chronological age *per se* explains desistance (see Rutter, 1989). The fact that chronological age remained in the model of desistance for males suggests, therefore, that the variables included in the models did not adequately cover the full range of potential influences on desistance.

References

Anderson, E. (1990). *'Streetwise: race, class and change in an urban community'*. Chicago: University of Chicago Press.

Aye Maung, N. (1995). *'Young people, victimisation and the police: British Crime Survey findings on experiences and attitudes of 12 to 15 year olds'*. Home Office Research Study, No. 140. London: HMSO.

Blumstein, A., Cohn, J., Roth, J.A. and Visher, C.A. (1986). *'Criminal careers and 'career criminals'*. Vols. I and II. Washington D.C.: National Academy of Sciences.

Bowling, B. (1990) *'Conceptual and Methodological Problems in Measuring 'Race' Differences in Delinquency'*. British Journal of Criminology, Vol. 30 No. 4, pp 483-493.

Bowling, B., Graham, J, and Ross, A. (1994) Self-reported offending among young people in England and Wales, in: Junger-Tas, J. Terlouw, J.G. and Klein, M. (Eds.) *'Delinquent behaviour among young people in the Western World: first results of the International Self-Report Delinquency Study'*. Amsterdam: Kugler.

Braithwaite, J. (1989). *'Crime, shame and reintegration'*. Cambridge: Cambridge University Press.

Brown, B.J. and McElrea, F.W.M. (Eds) (1994). *'The youth court in New Zealand: A model of new justice'*. Auckland: Legal Research Foundation.

Central Drugs Coordination Unit. (1994). *'Tackling drugs together'*. London: HMSO.

Children's Society. (1987). *'Young people under pressure'*. London: The Children's Society.

Chisholm, L. and Hurrelman, K. (1995). *'Adolescence in modern Europe. Pluralized transition patterns and their implications for personal and social risks'* Journal of Adolescence, Vol. 18, pp 129 – 158.

Department for Education. (1989a). *'Discipline in Schools'.* Committee of Inquiry chaired by Lord Elton. London: DES.

Department for Education. (1989b). *'Attendance at School'.* Education Observed 13. Her Majesty's Inspectorate. London: DES.

Department for Education. (1991). *'The Education Pupil Attendance Record Regulations'.* Circular 11/91. London: DfE.

Department for Education. (1994a). *'Pupil Behaviour and Discipline'.* Circular 8/94. London: DfE.

Department for Education. (1994b). *'Exclusions from School'.* Circular 10/94. London: DfE.

Department for Education. (1994c). *'School Attendance: Policy and Practice on Categorisation of Absence'.* London: DfE.

Department for Education. (1995). *'National survey of local education authorities'* policies and procedures for the identification of, and provision for, children who are out of school by reason of exclusion or otherwise'. London: DfE.

Department of Education & Science. (1983) *'Young People In The 1980s*, HMSO, London.

Douglas, J.W.B. (1964). *'The Home and the School'.* London: MacGibbon and Kee.

Douglas, J.W.B., Ross, J.M., Hammond, W.A. and Mulligan, D.G. (1966) *'Delinquency and social class'.* British Journal of Criminology. 6, pp 294-302.

Dryfoos, J.G. (1990). *'Adolescents at risk'.* New York: Oxford University Press.

Elliott, D.S. and Ageton, S. A. (1980) *'Reconciling Race and Class Differences in Self-Reported and Official Estimates of Delinquency'* American Sociological Review, Vol 45: pp 95-220.

Elliott, D.S. and Voss, H.L.(1974). *'Delinquency and Drop-out'.* Toronto:Lexington.

Farrington, D. P. (1986) *'Age and Crime'.* In: Tonry, M. and Morris, N. (Eds.), Crime and justice: An annual review of research. Vol. VII, pp 189-250. Chicago: University of Chicago Press.

Farrington, D. P. (1989). *'Self-reported and official offending from adolescence to adulthood'.* In: Klien, M.W. (Ed.) Cross-national research in self-reported crime and delinquency. Boston: Kluwer.

Farrington, D. P. (1992). *'Criminal career research in the United Kingdom'.* British Journal of Criminology. 32, no. 4, pp 521 – 536.

Farrington, D. P. (1994a) *'Human Development and Criminal Careers'.* In: Maguire, M., Morgan, R. and Reiner, R. (Eds.), The Oxford Handbook of Criminology. Oxford: Clarendon Press.

Farrington, D.P. (1994b). *'The nature and origins of delinquency'.* Jack Tizzard Memorial Lecture, 2nd European Conference of the Association for Child Psychology and Psychiatry, Winchester.

Gibbons, J. And Thorpe, S. (1990). *'Can Voluntary Support Projects Help Vulnerable Families? The Work of Home-Start'.* British Journal of Social Work. 19, pp. 189-202.

Gilchrist, R. and Jeffs, T. (1995). *'Foyers: Housing solution or folly?'* Youth and Policy, Autumn 1995, Issue no. 50.

Gove, W.R. and Crutchfield, R.D. (1982). 'The family and juvenile delinquency'. Sociological Quarterly 23, pp 301-319.

Graham, J. (1988). *'Schools, Disruptive Behaviour And Delinquency'.* Home Office Research Study, No. 96. London: HMSO.

Graham, J. (1989) *Families, parenting skills and delinquency.* Research Bulletin No. 26 1989. London: Home Office Research and Statistics Department.

Graham, J. (1990) *'Decarceration in the Federal Republic of Germany: How Practitioners are Succeeding Where Policy-makers have Failed'.* British Journal of Criminology, vol. 30, no. 2, pp 150 – 170.

Graham, J. (1992). *'The school'.* In: Family, school and community: towards a social crime prevention agenda. Swindon: Crime Concern.

Graham, J. and Utting, D. (1994). *'Families, schools and criminality prevention'.* Paper presented at the 22nd Cropwood Conference: Preventing crime and disorder. Cambridge: University of Cambridge.

Hagan, J. (1994). *'Crime and Disrepute'.* Thousand Oaks: Pine Forge Press.

Hagell, A. and Newburn, T. (1994) *'Persistent Young Offenders'*. London: Policy Studies Institute.

Hansen, D.A. (1986). *'Family-School Articulations: The Effects Of Interaction Rule Mismatch'*. American Educational Research Journal. 23, pp. 643-659.

Harris, N. (1988). *'Social Security and the Transition to Adulthood'*, Journal of Social Policy 17, 501-523.

Hindelang, M.J., Hirschi, T and Weis, J.G.H. (1981) *'Measuring Delinquency'*. Beverley Hills: Sage.

Hirschi, T. (1969) *'Causes of Delinquency'*, University of Chicago Press: Berkeley.

Hogan, D. P. and Astone, N. M. (1986) *'The Transition to Adulthood'*, Annual Review of Sociology, 12, pp 109-130.

Home Office. (1990). *'Partnership in crime prevention'*. London: HMSO.

Home Office. (1992) *'Race and the Criminal Justice System'*. London: Home Office.

Home Office. (1993) *'Information on the Criminal Justice System in England and Wales, Digest 2'*. London: Home Office Research and Statistics Department.

House of Commons Home Affairs Committee. (1993) *'Juvenile Offenders'*. Sixth Report. London: House Of Commons.

Johnson, R. E. (1987) *'Mother's versus father's role in causing delinquency'* Adolescence, Vol 22 No. 86 pp 305-315.

Junger, M. (1989) *'Discrepancies Between Police and Self-Report Data for Dutch Racial Minorities'*, British Journal of Criminology Vol. 29 No. 3 pp 273-284.

Junger-Tas, J. (1988) *'Causal Factors: Social Control Theory'*. In: Junger-Tas, J. and Block, R. (Eds.) Juvenile Delinquency in the Netherlands. Berkeley: Kugler Publications.

Junger-Tas, J (1993) *'Changes in the Family and their Impact on Delinquency'*. European Journal of Criminal Policy and Research, Vol 1 No.1 pp 27-51.

Junger-Tas, J. Terlouw, J.G. and Klein, M. (Eds.) (1994) *Delinquent behaviour among young people in the Western World: first results of the International Self-Report Delinquency Study.* Amsterdam: Kugler.

Kazdin, A.E. (1985) *'Treatment Of Anti-Social Behaviour In Children And Adolescents'.* Homewood, Il: Dorsey.

Kelly, S. (1992). *'The Family'.* In: Family, school and community: towards a social crime prevention agenda. Swindon: Crime Concern.

Killeen, D. (1992). *'Leaving home: housing and income – social policy on leaving home.'* In: Coleman, J.C. and Warren-Adamson, C. (Eds) Youth Policy in the 1990s: the way forward. London: Routledge.

Knight, B. J. and West D. J. (1975) *'Temporary and Continuing Delinquency'.* British Journal of Criminology Vol 15. No.1 pp 43-166.

Kolvin, I. Miller, F.J.W. Scott, D.M. Gatzanis, S.R.M. and Fleeting, M. (1990). *'Continuities Of Deprivation? The Newcastle 1000 Family Study'.* Aldershot: Avebury.

Laub, J. H. and Sampson, R. J. (1993) *'Turning Points in the Life Course: Why Change Matters to the Study of Crime'.* Criminology Vol 31 No 3.

Leffert, N. and Petersen, A.C. (1995) *'Patterns of Development During Adolescence'.* In: Rutter, M. and Smith, D. (Eds.): Psychosocial Disorders in Young People: Time Trends and their Causes. Chichester: John Wiley.

Leitner, M., Shapland, J. and Wiles, P. (1993) *'Drug Usage and Drugs Prevention: The Views and Habits of the General Public'.* Report Prepared for the Home Office Drugs Prevention Initiative. London: HMSO.

Lindstrom, P. (1993). *'School and Delinquency in a Contextual Perspective'.* Stockholm: National Council For Crime Prevention.

Loeber, R. and Stouthamer-Loeber, M. (1986). *'Family Factors As Correlates And Predictors Of Juvenile Conduct Problems And Delinquency'.* In: Tonry, M. And Morris, N. (Eds): Crime And Justice – An Annual Review Of Research. Vol.7, University Of Chicago.

Lovey, J., Docking, J. and Evans, R. (1993). *'Exclusion from School: Provision for Disaffection in Key Stage 4'.* London: Roehampton Institute.

Marshall, I.H. and Webb, V.J. (1992) *'Omaha ISRD Pilot Study'* Paper presented at the meeting of the International Self-report Delinquency Project, The Hague, The Netherlands.

Martin, F.M., Fox, S.J. and Murray, K. (1981). *'Children out of court'*. Edinburgh: Scottish Academic Press.

Mayhew, P. and Elliott, D. (1990) *'Self-Reported Offending, Victimization and the British Crime Survey'*. Violence and Victims. Vol. 5 No.2.

Mortimore, P., Sammons, P., Stoll, L., Lewis, D. and Ecob, R. (1988). *'School Matters: The Junior Years'*. Shepton Mallett: Open Books.

Mott, J. and Mirrlees-Black, C. (1995). *'Self-Reported Drug Misuse in England and Wales: Findings from the 1992 British Crime Survey'*. Home Office Research and Planning Unit Paper, No. 89. London: Home Office.

MVA Consultancy. (1991). *'Links Between Truancy And Delinquency'*. Report Prepared For The Scottish Office Education Department.

NACRO. (1977). *'Homelessness and offending'*. London: NACRO.

OPCS. (1994). *'Population Trends'*. No. 77, Autumn 1994. Government Statistical Service: HMSO.

Parker, H. (1976) *'Boys Will be Men'*. In Mungham, G. & Pearson, G. (Eds) (1976) Working Class Youth Culture. London: Routledge.

Parker, H., Jarvis, G. and Sumner, M. (1989). *'Unmasking the magistrates: the 'custody or not' decision in sentencing young offenders'*. Milton Keynes: Open University Press.

Rand, A. (1987) *'Transitional Life Events & Desistance from Delinquency & Crime'*. In: Wolfgang, M. E. & Thornberry, T. P and Figlio, R. M. (Eds). From Boy to Man, From Delinquency to Crime.

Reid, J.B. (1993). *'Prevention Of Conduct Disorder Before And After School Entry: Relating Interventions To Developmental Findings'*. Development And Psychopathology. 5, pp. 243-262.

Riley, J. and Shaw, M. (1985) *'Parental Supervision and Juvenile Delinquency'* Home Office Research Study No. 83. London: HMSO.

Robins, L.N. (1966). *'Deviant Children Grown Up'*. New York: Robert E. Krieger.

Rutherford, A. (1992) *'Growing Out of Crime: The New Era'.* London: Waterside Press.

Rutter, M. (1989) *'Age as an ambiguous variable in developmental research: Some epidemiological considerations from developmental psychopathology'.* International Journal of Behavioural Development 12, pp 1-134.

Rutter, M., Maughan, B., Mortimore, P. and Ouston, J. (1979). *'Fifteen Thousand Hours: Secondary Schools And Their Effects On Children'.* London: Open Books.

Rutter, M and Giller, H. (1983) *'Juvenile Delinquency: Trends and Perspectives'.* Harmondsworth: Penguin.

Sampson, R. J. and Laub, J. H. (1993).*'Crime in the Making: Pathways and Turning Points Through Life'.* Cambridge, Mass: Harvard University Press.

Shover, N. (1983) *'The Later Stages of Ordinary Property Offenders' Careers',* Social Problems, 31, pp 208-218.

Shover, N. (1985) *'Aging Criminals',* Sage: London.

Smith, D. J. (1995) *'Youth Crime and Conduct Disorders'.* In: Rutter, M. and Smith, D. (Eds.): Psychosocial Disorders in Young People: Time Trends and their Causes. Chichester: John Wiley.

Tarling, R. (1993) *'Analysing Offending; Data, Models and Interpretations',* London: HMSO.

Tuck, M. (1989). *'Drinking and disorder: A study of non-metropolitan violence'.* Home Office Research Study, 108. London: HMSO.

Utting, D., Bright, J., and Henricson, C. (1993). *'Crime And The Family'.* Family Policy Studies Centre. Occasional Paper 16. London.

Wadsworth, M. (1979). *'The Roots Of Delinquency'.* Oxford: Martin Robertson.

Wallace, C. (1987) *'For Richer, For Poorer: Growing Up In & Out of Work'.* Tavistock: London.

Walmsley, R., Howard, L. and White, S. (1991). *'The National Prison Survey 1991: Main Findings'.* Home Office Research Study No. 128. London: HMSO.

Warr, M. (1993). *'Parents, peers and delinquency'.* Social Forces, 72(1), pp 247-264.

West, D. and Farrington, D. P. (1973) *'Who Becomes Delinquent?'*, London: Heinemann.

West, D. and Farrington, D. P. (1977) *'The Delinquent Way of Life'*, London: Heinemann.

Wilson, H.(1980). *'Parental Supervision: A Neglected Aspect Of Delinquency'.* British Journal Of Criminology. 20, No.3, pp. 203-235.

Publications

List of Research and Planning Unit Publications

The Research and Planning Unit (previously the Research Unit) has been publishing its work since 1955, and a list of reports for the last three years is provided below. A **full** list of publications is available on request from the Research and Planning Unit.

Home Office Research Studies (HORS)

125. **Magistrates' court or Crown Court? Mode of trial decisions and sentencing.** Carol Hedderman and David Moxon. 1992. vii + 53pp. (0 11 341036 0).

126. **Developments in the use of compensation orders in magistrates' courts since October 1988.** David Moxon, John Martin Corkery and Carol Hedderman. 1992. x + 48pp. (0 11 341042 5).

127. **A comparative study of firefighting arrangements in Britain, Denmark, the Netherlands and Sweden.** John Graham, Simon Field, Roger Tarling and Heather Wilkinson. 1992. x + 57pp. (0 11 341043 3).

128. **The National Prison Survey 1991: main findings.** Roy Walmsley, Liz Howard and Sheila White. 1992. xiv + 82pp. (0 11 341051 4).

129. **Changing the Code: police detention under the revised PACE Codes of Practice.** David Brown, Tom Ellis and Karen Larcombe. 1992. viii + 122pp. (0 11 341052 2).

130. **Car theft: the offender's perspective.** Roy Light, Claire Nee and Helen Ingham. 1993. x + 89pp. (0 11 341069 7).

131. **Housing, Community and Crime: The Impact of the Priority Estates Project.** Janet Foster and Timothy Hope with assistance from Lizanne Dowds and Mike Sutton. 1993. xi + 118pp. (0 11 341078 6).

132. **The 1992 British Crime Survey.** Pat Mayhew, Natalie Aye Maung and Catriona Mirrlees-Black. 1993. xiii + 206pp. (0 11 341094 8).

133. **Intensive Probation in England and Wales: an evaluation.** George Mair, Charles Lloyd, Claire Nee and Rae Sibbett. 1994. xiv + 143pp. (0 11 341114 6).

134. **Contacts between Police and Public: findings from the 1992 British Crime Survey.** Wesley G Skogan. 1995. ix + 93pp. (0 11 341115 4).

135. **Policing low-level disorder : Police use of Section 5 of the Public Order Act 1986.** David Brown and Tom Ellis. 1994. ix + 69pp. (0 11 341116 2).

136. **Explaining reconviction rates: A critical analysis.** Charles Lloyd, George Mair and Mike Hough. 1995. xiv + 103pp. (0 11 341117 0).

137. **Case Screening by the Crown Prosecution Service: How and why cases are terminated.** Debbie Crisp and David Moxon. 1995. viii + 66pp. (0 11 341137 5).

138. **Public Interest Case Assessment Schemes.** Debbie Crisp, Claire Whittaker and Jessica Harris. 1995. x + 58pp. (0 11 341139 1).

139. **Policing domestic violence in the 1990s.** Sharon Grace. 1995. x + 74pp. (0 11 341140 5).

140. **Young people, victimisation and the police: British Crime Survey findings on experiences and attitudes of 12 to 15 year olds.** Natalie Aye Maung. xii + 140pp. (Not yet published)

141. **The Settlement of refugees in Britain.** Jenny Carey-Wood, Karen Duke, Valerie Karn and Tony Marshall. 1995. xii + 133pp. (0 11 341145 6).

142. **Vietnamese Refugees since 1982.** Karen Duke and Tony Marshall. 1995. x + 62pp. (0 11 341147 2).

143. **The Parish Special Constables Scheme.** Peter Southgate, Tom Bucke and Carole Byron. 1995. x + 59pp. (1 85893 458 3).

144. **Measuring the Satisfaction of the Courts with the Probation Service.** Chris May. 1995. x + 76pp. (1 85893 483 4).

Research and Planning Unit Papers (RPUP)

65. **Offending while on bail: a survey of recent studies.** Patricia M. Morgan. 1992.

66. **Juveniles sentenced for serious offences: a comparison of regimes in Young Offender Institutions and Local Authority Community Homes.** John Ditchfield and Liza Catan. 1992.

67. **The management and deployment of police armed response vehicles.** Peter Southgate. 1992.

68. **Using psychometric personality tests in the selection of firearms officers.** Catriona Mirrlees-Black. 1992.

69. **Bail information schemes: practice and effect.** Charles Lloyd. 1992.

70. **Crack and cocaine in England and Wales.** Joy Mott (editor). 1992.

71. **Rape: from recording to conviction.** Sharon Grace, Charles Lloyd and Lorna J. F. Smith. 1992.

72. **The National Probation Survey 1990.** Chris May. 1993.

73. **Public satisfaction with police services.** Peter Southgate and Debbie Crisp. 1993.

74. **Disqualification from driving: an effective penalty?** Catriona Mirrlees-Black. 1993.

75. **Detention under the Prevention of Terrorism (Temporary Provisions) Act 1989: Access to legal advice and outside contact.** David Brown. 1993.

76. **Panel assessment schemes for mentally disordered offenders.** Carol Hedderman. 1993.

77. **Cash-limiting the probation service: a case study in resource allocation.** Simon Field and Mike Hough. 1993.

78. **The probation response to drug misuse.** Claire Nee and Rae Sibbitt. 1993.

79   **Approval of rifle and target shooting clubs: the effects of the new and revised criteria.** John Martin Corkery. 1993.

80.   **The long-term needs of victims: A review of the literature.** Tim Newburn. 1993.

81.   **The welfare needs of unconvicted prisoners.** Diane Caddle and Sheila White. 1994.

82.   **Racially motivated crime: a British Crime Survey analysis.** Natalie Aye Maung and Catriona Mirrlees-Black. 1994.

83.   **Mathematical models for forecasting Passport demand.** Andy Jones and John MacLeod. 1994.

84.   **The theft of firearms**. John Corkery. 1994.

85.   **Equal opportunities and the Fire Service.** Tom Bucke. 1994.

86.   **Drug Education Amongst Teenagers: a 1992 British Crime Survey Analysis**. Lizanne Dowds and Judith Redfern. 1995.

87.   **Group 4 Prisoner Escort Service: a survey of customer satisfaction.** Claire Nee. 1994.

88.   **Special Considerations: Issues for the Management and Organisation of the Volunteer Police.** Catriona Mirrlees-Black and Carole Byron. 1995.

89.   **Self-reported drug misuse in England and Wales: findings from the 1992 British Crime Survey.** Joy Mott and Catriona Mirrlees-Black. 1995.

90.   **Improving bail decisions: the bail process project, phase 1.** John Burrows, Paul Henderson and Patricia Morgan. 1995.

91.   **Practitioners' views of the Criminal Justice Act: a survey of criminal justice agencies.** George Mair and Chris May. 1995.

92.   **Obscene, threatening and other troublesome telephone calls to women in England and Wales: 1982-1992.** Wendy Buck, Michael Chatterton and Ken Pease. 1995.

93.   **A survey of the prisoner escort and custody service provided by Group 4 and by Securicor Custodial Services.** Diane Caddle. 1995.

Research Findings

1. **Magistrates' court or Crown Court? Mode of trial decisions and their impact on sentencing.** Carol Hedderman and David Moxon. 1992.

2. **Surveying crime: findings from the 1992 British Crime Survey.** Pat Mayhew and Natalie Aye Maung. 1992.

3. **Car Theft: the offenders' perspective.** Claire Nee. 1993.

4. **The National Prison Survey 1991: main findings.** Roy Walmsley, Liz Howard and Sheila White. 1993.

5. **Changing the Code: Police detention under the revised PACE codes of practice.** David Brown, Tom Ellis and Karen Larcombe. 1993.

6. **Rifle and pistol target shooting clubs: The effects of new approval criteria.** John M. Corkery. 1993.

7. **Self-reported drug misuse in England and Wales. Main findings from the 1992 British Crime Survey.** Joy Mott and Catriona Mirrlees-Black. 1993.

8. **Findings from the International Crime Survey.** Pat Mayhew. 1994.

9   **Fear of Crime: Findings from the 1992 British Crime Survey.** Catriona Mirrlees-Black and Natalie Aye Maung. 1994.

10. **Does the Criminal Justice system treat men and women differently?** Carol Hedderman and Mike Hough. 1994.

11. **Participation in Neighbourhood Watch: Findings from the 1992 British Crime Survey.** Lizanne Dowds and Pat Mayhew. 1994.

12. **Explaining Reconviction Rates: A Critical Analysis.** Charles Lloyd, George Mair and Mike Hough. 1995.

13. **Equal opportunities and the Fire Service.** Tom Bucke. 1994.

14. **Trends in Crime: Findings from the 1994 British Crime Survey.** Pat Mayhew, Catriona Mirrlees-Black and Natalie Aye Maung. 1994.

15. **Intensive Probation in England and Wales: an evaluation.** George Mair, Charles Lloyd, Claire Nee and Rae Sibbett. 1995.

16. **The settlement of refugees in Britain.** Jenny Carey-Wood, Karen Duke, Valerie Karn and Tony Marshall. 1995.

17. **Young people, victimisation and the police: British Crime Survey findings on experiences and attitudes of 12 to 15 year olds.** Natalie Aye Maung. (Not yet published)

18. **Vietnamese Refugees since 1982.** Karen Duke and Tony Marshall. 1995.

19. **Supervision of Restricted Patients in the Community.** Dell and Grounds. (Not yet published)

20. **Videotaping children's evidence: an evaluation.** Graham Davies, Clare Wilson, Rebecca Mitchell and John Milsom. 1995.

Research Bulletin

The Research Bulletin is published twice each year and contains short articles on recent research. Research Bulletin No. 37 was published recently.

Occasional Papers

Coping with a crisis: the introduction of three and two in a cell. T. G. Weiler. 1992.

Psychiatric Assessment at the Magistrates' Court. Philip Joseph. 1992.

Measurement of caseload weightings in magistrates' courts. Richard J. Gadsden and Graham J. Worsdale. 1992.

The CDE of scheduling in magistrates' courts. John W. Raine and Michael J. Willson. 1992.

Employment opportunities for offenders. David Downes. 1993.

Sex offenders: a framework for the evaluation of community-based treatment. Mary Barker and Rod Morgan. 1993.

Suicide attempts and self-injury in male prisons. Alison Liebling and Helen Krarup. 1993.

Measurement of caseload weightings associated with the Children Act. Richard J. Gadsden and Graham J. Worsdale. 1994. (Available from the RPU Information Section.)

Managing difficult prisoners: The Lincoln and Hull special units. Professor Keith Bottomley, Professor Norman Jepson, Mr Kenneth Elliott and Dr Jeremy Coid. 1994. (Available from RPU Information Section).

The Nacro diversion iniative for mentally disturbed offenders: an account and an evaluation. Home Office, NACRO and Mental Health Foundation. 1994. (Available from RPU Information Section.)

Probation Motor Projects in England and Wales. J P Martin and Douglas Martin. 1994.

Community-based treatment of sex offenders: an evaluation of seven treatment programmes. R Beckett, A Beech, D Fisher and A S Fordham. 1994.

Videotaping children's evidence: an evaluation. Graham Davies, Clare Wilson, Rebecca Mitchell and John Milsom. 1995

Books

Analysing Offending. Data, Models and Interpretations. Roger Tarling. 1993. viii + 203pp. (0 11 341080 8).

Requests for Publications

Home Office Research Studies from 143 onwards, *Research and Planning Unit Papers, Research Findings, the Research and Planning Unit Programme and Research Bulletins* are available on request from the Information Section, Home Office Research and Planning Unit, Room 278, 50 Queen Anne's Gate, London SW1H 9AT. Telephone: 0171 273 2084 (answering machine).

Occasional Papers can be purchased from: Home Office, Publications Unit, 50 Queen Anne's Gate, London SW1 9AT. Telephone: 0171 273 2302.

Home Office Research Studies prior to 143 can be purchased from:

HMSO Publications Centre
(Mail, fax and telephone orders only)
PO Box 276, London SW8 5DT
Telephone orders: 0171-873 9090
General enquiries: 0171-873 0011
(queuing system in operation for both numbers)
Fax orders: 0171-873 8200

And also from **HMSO Bookshops**